**New Directions for
Community Colleges**

Arthur M. Cohen
EDITOR-IN-CHIEF

Florence B. Brawer
ASSOCIATE EDITOR

Carrie B. Kisker
MANAGING EDITOR

# Critical Thinking:
# Unfinished Business

Christine M. McMahon
EDITOR

Number 130 • Summer 2005
Jossey-Bass
San Francisco

CRITICAL THINKING: UNFINISHED BUSINESS
*Christine M. McMahon* (ed.)
New Directions for Community Colleges, no. 130

*Arthur M. Cohen,* Editor-in-Chief
*Florence B. Brawer,* Associate Editor

NEW DIRECTIONS FOR COMMUNITY COLLEGES (ISSN 0194-3081, electronic ISSN 1536-0733) is part of The Jossey-Bass Higher and Adult Education Series and is published quarterly by Wiley Subscription Services, Inc., A Wiley Company, at Jossey-Bass, 989 Market Street, San Francisco, California 94103-1741. Periodicals Postage Paid at San Francisco, California, and at additional mailing offices. POSTMASTER: Send address changes to New Directions for Community Colleges, Jossey-Bass, 989 Market Street, San Francisco, California 94103-1741.

SUBSCRIPTIONS cost $80.00 for individuals and $170.00 for institutions, agencies, and libraries. Prices subject to change. See order form in back of book.

EDITORIAL CORRESPONDENCE should be sent to the Editor-in-Chief, Arthur M. Cohen, at the Graduate School of Education and Information Studies, University of California, Box 951521, Los Angeles, California 90095-1521. All manuscripts receive anonymous reviews by external referees.

*New Directions for Community Colleges* is indexed in Current Index to Journals in Education (ERIC).

Microfilm copies of issues and articles are available in 16mm and 35mm, as well as microfiche in 105mm, through University Microfilms Inc., 300 North Zeeb Road, Ann Arbor, Michigan 48106-1346.

# CONTENTS

# EDITOR'S NOTES

The concept of critical thinking has found its way into course descriptions, textbook titles, and even college mission statements. Yet far from being satisfied with these successes, scholars in the field believe that much unfinished business remains: critical thinking has not found its way into many classrooms. Studies show that, with the exception of a few best-practice examples, critical thinking—in our highly selective universities and our community colleges—is being neither effectively taught nor even correctly understood. Even many faculty who believe that they are teaching it are not succeeding. The solution to this widely unrecognized problem lies in the entire academic community coming to understand a substantive definition of critical thinking, and then developing and implementing professional development plans that engage not only the faculty but all members of the campus community.

This volume of *New Directions for Community Colleges* (*NDCC*) presents blueprints for such plans, best practices from colleges that have already begun to implement such plans, and methods for assessing programs that emerge from them. Finally, the volume connects the teaching of critical thinking to the Learning College, an idea developed by Terry O'Banion, president of the League for Innovation in the Community College, that calls on institutions to place learning first by offering multiple options for learning and documenting that students demonstrate improved learning.

Chapter One, by Cynthia Barnes, takes a historical perspective on critical thinking in the community college by revisiting the critical thinking programs described in her 1992 *NDCC* volume titled "Critical Thinking: Educational Imperative." Some of these programs have remained true to their missions, yet Barnes reports that although colleges often cite critical thinking as a key objective, common classroom practice does not generally reflect its importance. She argues for the need to change how we teach and describes a learner-centered model for professional development that holds promise for revolutionizing the teaching of critical thinking in community college classrooms.

Chapter Two, by Trudy Bers, addresses the all-important issue of assessment and gives a comprehensive review of assessment techniques and standardized tests suitable for assessing critical thinking in the community college. She notes that much work remains to be done in this area.

Chapter Three, by Richard Paul, argues that critical thinking is neither correctly understood nor effectively taught in the majority of colleges and universities. He defines a substantive concept of critical thinking and urges colleges to take measures to ensure that students actually learn to think critically.

Chapter Four, by Linda Elder, proposes a solution to the problems raised by the first three chapters: a detailed plan for a professional development program that is based on a substantive definition of critical thinking. She illustrates this solution by describing the new critical thinking program at Surry Community College (North Carolina), which has recognized and incorporated the link between critical thinking and the Learning College.

Chapter Five, by Stephen Brookfield, examines one cause of the failure to teach critical thinking successfully: student resistance. He examines reasons for this resistance to critical thinking and offers specific suggestions for overcoming it.

Chapter Six, by Gerald Nosich, extends the argument for change by examining two common models of community college teaching: incorporating critical thinking activities as just one of many teaching techniques, and trying to cover as much disciplinary content as possible. He argues that both models are counterproductive and suggests instead that instructors teach students a few central concepts in each discipline, focusing on how those concepts fit together to form a coherent system and how the discipline tries to address these questions. Chapter Seven, by Jerry Herman, also lays out recommendations for effectively teaching critical thinking, by describing a course he developed at Laney College, a large urban community college in Oakland, California. He includes in the chapter specific assignments and classroom instructions that can be implemented at other community colleges across the country.

Chapters Eight and Nine describe two critical thinking programs at neighboring community colleges in Maryland. The programs have been in existence for years but have taken divergent paths. Chapter Eight, by William Peirce, discusses the newly implemented "Year of Critical Thinking" at Prince George's Community College, an effort to improve critical thinking that encompasses all departments and courses. Chapter Nine, by Francine Jamin and Marcia Bronstein, describes how Montgomery College has moved its critical thinking activities into the community through its "Jefferson Cafés," gatherings in which students, faculty, and members of the community get together to discuss short readings that are distributed to prospective participants several weeks prior to the Café.

Chapter Ten, by Shannon Calderone, offers key information and resources for community college educators interested in making effective teaching of critical thinking a reality on their campus.

Taken together, these chapters paint an unsettling picture of the current state of critical thinking in today's community colleges, yet they also offer hope as well as specific recommendations for the future. Even though the academic world agrees that critical thinking is important, by and large it is not happening in all community college classrooms and, when it does happen, is not being assessed as it should. It seems that the business of critical thinking is, indeed, unfinished. Nonetheless, the experts who contributed to this volume agree that—given time and substantial administrative commitment—it is possible to teach critical thinking. Their chapters offer models for classroom practice, as well as advice and examples for creating and sustaining successful professional development programs. Teaching critical thinking to community college students may indeed be unfinished business, but it need not remain so. Making it a reality is possible, and certainly business of the highest importance.

Christine M. McMahon
Editor

CHRISTINE M. MCMAHON *is retired from Montgomery College in Rockville, Maryland, where she taught English and directed the Critical Literacy program during the early 1990s. She is a coauthor of* Critical Thinking, Thoughtful Writing *and is currently teaching at City College of San Francisco.*

1

*More than a decade ago, community colleges across the nation mobilized legions of faculty to craft critical thinking initiatives on their campus. Were these initiatives simply the latest educational fad, or did the implementation provoke substantive, lasting changes not only in what we teach but in how we teach?*

# Critical Thinking Revisited: Its Past, Present, and Future

*Cynthia A. Barnes*

In the mid-1980s, when the Community College of Aurora, Colorado (CCA) tapped me to lead its cutting-edge critical thinking initiative, called the Integrated Thinking Skills Project, I was enthusiastic and deeply hopeful that, somehow, I could coalesce our faculty into scholar-practitioners who would serve as catalysts for substantively changing not only *what* we taught but *how* we taught.

As I think back now, more than a decade later, I ponder the efforts of the first group of faculty engaged in the Integrated Thinking Skills Project. As we struggled through Bruce Tuckman's model (1965) whereby groups first "form" politely, then "storm" through differences of opinion in order to normalize relationships, and ultimately "perform" as a cohesive group, we initially maintained our stance that, of course, we were "doing" critical thinking. Eventually we found out that we, as faculty, were indeed doing critical thinking, but our students were doing something else: transferring the instructors' notes into their own, without putting too much thought into any of it.

We discovered along our difficult journey that although *we* might have actually been doing some critical thinking in our disciplines, our students were doing little more than continuing their trek through what I have dubbed the "teacher as God syndrome." What our students were doing, in effect, was guessing what faculty wanted so they could successfully regurgitate it on Scantron tests, only to leave our classroom untaught, and more important unlearned.

NEW DIRECTIONS FOR COMMUNITY COLLEGES, no. 130, Summer 2005 © Wiley Periodicals, Inc.

This collective—even paradigm-shattering—realization fueled our effort to infuse our courses with the teaching of and for critical thinking. Our excitement about the possibility of changing the world—populating it with educated, informed citizens whom we could teach to think critically (which comes from the Greek word *kritikos,* which means "to question") about any subject we taught—sustained our fear-filled steps through this altogether new process. Instead of teaching as we ourselves had been taught, we were embarking on a brand-new journey: guiding our students through the mysteries deeply embedded in the subjects we had for years so inveterately "taught."

Our efforts at CCA eventually changed our teaching and learning climate and culture. As we developed and implemented our project, we formulated an ongoing, comprehensive professional development model (to be outlined later in this chapter) that fully engaged faculty in their own learning and helped us build a learner-centered curriculum infusion process. The initiative became so widespread and successful that students began to complain to the dean when their instructors persisted in lecturing them from decades-worn, laminated, yellow legal-pad notes.

The Integrated Thinking Skills Project at CCA was but one of many community college initiatives designed to teach students to think critically about academic subjects. But what happened to the many critical thinking initiatives undertaken across the nation at the same time? Were they able to effect systemic change not only in the *what* but also in the *how* of college teaching? Did their efforts weather the test of time, or did they vanish once funding ran out? What vestiges of the community college's inaugural efforts to teach critical thinking remain?

This chapter looks back over the past thirteen years of critical thinking in community colleges and asks both what we have learned and what is still left to do. It then revisits some of the prominent programs that emerged in community colleges more than a decade ago, taking a snapshot of how they have evolved. The chapter concludes by presenting a professional development model for the teaching and learning of critical thinking, which is based on what the Community College of Aurora learned through its Integrated Thinking Skills Project.

## Critical Thinking Today

More than many other educational innovations, critical thinking has not only persisted but has inserted itself into the fabric and fiber of many community college missions and, more important, practices. It has "taken root" (Weinstein, 1995, n.p.). Unlike other educational fads, it has infiltrated educational literature and, to some extent, community college teaching and learning practice: "Critical thinking is perhaps the most oft-cited postsecondary learning objective, although common classroom practice belies its importance" (Browne and Meuti, 1999, p. 162).

Critical thinking, no longer confined to isolated philosophy courses in college catalogues, has seeped into such academic disciplines as cognitive psychology, philosophy, behavioral psychology, and educational psychology (Huitt, 1998). "These changing conditions require new outcomes, such as critical thinking, to be included as a focus of schooling. Old standards of simply being able to score well on a standardized test of basic skills, though still appropriate, cannot be the sole means by which we judge the academic success or failure of our students" (Huitt, 1998, n.p.).

Tens of thousands of books, articles, Internet sites, and monographs about critical thinking jam traditional and electronic libraries, bookstores, and media. As well, few colleges in the country would not feature critical thinking as an essential component of a successful collegiate experience. Indeed, philosophy, humanities, and other critical thinking courses are listed in college catalogues across the nation. Critical thinking programs and projects are still funded and in full swing at schools such as Longview Community College (Missouri), Surry Community College (North Carolina), and Miami-Dade Community College (Florida).

## Revisiting Critical Thinking Programs

In 1992, Jossey-Bass published a *New Directions for Community Colleges* sourcebook titled "Critical Thinking: Educational Imperative" (Barnes, 1992), which detailed initiatives at community colleges across the country. The book's contributors discussed infusing critical thinking into writing and humanities courses at Cuyahoga Community College (Ohio) and embedding critical thinking into the social sciences at Tidewater Community College (Virginia), presented across-the-curriculum efforts such as the Critical Literacy Project at Oakton Community College (Illinois) and learner-centered strategies for teaching critical thinking at several Minnesota community colleges, and outlined specific techniques for critical thinking used by occupational and technical faculty to prepare students for the workplace.

One chapter (Chaffee, 1992) featured the Critical Thought Skills course, the keystone class taught by faculty from various disciplines that propelled the critical thinking movement at LaGuardia Community College (New York). The LaGuardia model, structured around paired courses where students took the keystone course along with another from a second discipline, gave students the opportunity to think critically about the content of both courses. Faculty discussed student progress at regular meetings, and they developed and practiced teaching methods that fostered critical thinking.

The 1992 volume also included a chapter on assessment of critical thinking, stemming from work done at Alverno College (Wisconsin), an innovator in the field of performance-based education. At Alverno, critical thinking was fostered through an ongoing process that helped students use the analytical frameworks of a particular discipline, provided opportunities for students to practice and refine their critical thinking skills, assessed critical thinking in the context of course content, gave students regular feedback based on explicit criteria, and encouraged faculty to work with others within and outside their discipline in order to sustain critical thinking as an institutional value and goal (Cromwell, 1992).

Of the six grant-funded critical thinking initiatives touted in the 1992 volume, three vanished when their funding ceased, three have continued, and two (those at LaGuardia and Alverno) have evolved and grown. The next section revisits these two programs and examines what has helped to sustain them.

**LaGuardia Community College.** John Chaffee, founder of the Critical Thought Skills project at LaGuardia Community College, believes that the critical thinking "movement" infused the concept into the national educational vocabulary. Currently head of the philosophy department at LaGuardia, Chaffee reports that critical thinking has become a key part of the infrastructure at his and other postsecondary institutions. LaGuardia offers, on average, a hundred philosophy and critical thinking courses per year, taught by full-time and adjunct faculty. A yearlong faculty seminar in teaching critical thinking is "going strong," and the Critical Thought Skills courses Chaffee put in place more than a decade ago have become an integral part of LaGuardia curricula (John Chaffee, personal communication, Sept. 2004).

Having an avid champion for critical thinking helped LaGuardia sustain its early efforts. In addition, the Critical Thought Skills courses developed at LaGuardia engaged faculty from a variety of disciplines. This cross-disciplinary focus ultimately integrated critical thinking into a variety of subject areas and gave faculty an opportunity to critically examine their own disciplines and build networks across disciplinary lines.

Another factor that helped sustain this program is that information about LaGuardia's work in critical thinking spread outside the institution. Through publications, conference presentations, and workshops, the value of LaGuardia's effort was recognized by other community colleges, which helped further embed critical thinking as an integral part of the LaGuardia college experience.

In Chaffee's view, the current state of critical thinking is a positive one. As he states, before the critical thinking initiatives of the 1980s and 1990s few people—except perhaps philosophy faculty teaching logic courses—had anything to do with critical thinking. As a result of those early efforts, however, most colleges worth their accreditation view critical thinking as a "core competency" that all students and graduates should possess. The early critical thinking efforts encouraged institutions to examine the kinds of competencies graduates would need for future success, and critical thinking emerged as a skill that should be an institutional focus (Chaffee, personal communication, Sept. 2004).

**Alverno College.** A pioneer in learner-centered instruction and assessment, Alverno College continues to promote critical thinking as a major collegiate outcome for students and now uses the Diagnostic Digital Portfolio as a hallmark of its "assessment-as-learning process" (Alverno College, 2003). As Huitt writes, "The movement to the information age has focused attention on good thinking as an important element of life success" (1998, n.p.). At Alverno, the emphasis on critical thinking as a lifelong learning competency has become a key component of the college's institutional mission.

As a result of Alverno's focus on critical thinking, faculty found themselves continuously involved in a process of examining what they were teaching and what students were learning. This focus on ability-based learning helped faculty coalesce into a community of learners themselves. This learning community was then the impetus for faculty to critically examine the content of their disciplines and, as a result, hone their own critical thinking abilities. Having experienced firsthand how this approach cemented long-term learning, rather than mere subject-matter regurgitation, Alverno faculty realized how critical it is to actively engage their students in this same process. As at LaGuardia, the cross-disciplinary immersion of critical thinking into the curriculum seems to be a key component to institutionalizing its teaching.

Since multiple assessments, including self-assessment, have long been a feature of the Alverno curriculum, the college now uses digital portfolios to give students and faculty more effective ways to demonstrate and assess learning. Alverno's ability-based learning model requires students to examine both what they learn and *how* they learn, and the digital portfolios provide students with the kind of ongoing feedback that spurs continuous improvement.

## Teaching for Critical Thinking

Critical thinking programs that have grown and flourished—such as those at LaGuardia and Alverno—have been characterized by three essentials: a forward-thinking champion, cross-disciplinary immersion, and solid documentation of success that spreads beyond the campus walls. But as we found at CCA those many years ago, the prospect of changing how we teach can mean a lot of work and is often a major barrier to the teaching of and for critical thinking. For example, "Just holding an instructional workshop is by itself of little worth" (Browne and Meuti, 1999, p. 163). If knowledge dispensation through lecture remains the major thrust of college teaching, there will be little time or room for teaching students to think critically. Similarly, if instructor-centered approaches to college teaching persist, students will neither learn the content of our disciplines nor learn to think critically about them.

As many community college faculty have come to learn, "thinking is not a spectator sport" (Halpern, 1996, back cover). Until and unless community

**3**

*Research demonstrates that most college faculty lack a
substantive concept of critical thinking, though they
mistakenly think otherwise. This chapter spells out the
implications of such a robust concept and emphasizes that
success in bringing a substantive concept of critical
thinking to college faculty requires well-planned, long-
term professional development based explicitly on the
multiple dimensions of a substantive concept of critical
thinking.*

# The State of Critical Thinking Today

*Richard Paul*

> Too many facts, too little conceptualizing, too much memorizing,
> and too little thinking.
>
> —Paul Hurd

What is the current state of critical thinking in higher education? Sadly,
studies demonstrate three disturbing, but hardly novel, facts: (1) most college faculty at all levels lack a substantive concept of critical thinking; (2)
most faculty don't realize they lack a substantive concept and instead
believe they understand critical thinking sufficiently and are already successfully teaching it within their discipline; (3) despite "reform" efforts,
lecture, rote memorization, and (largely ineffective) short-term study
strategies are still the norm in college instruction and learning today (Paul,
Elder, and Bartell, 1997).

   These three facts, taken together, represent a serious obstacle to essential, long-term institutional change, because only when administrative and
faculty leaders grasp the nature, implications, and power of a robust concept of critical thinking, as well as the negative implications of its absence,
will they be able to orchestrate a substantive professional development program. When faculty have a vague notion of critical thinking, or when they
reduce it to a single-discipline model (as in teaching critical thinking
through a "logic" or a "study skills" course), they are largely unable to identify ineffective teaching practices or develop more effective ones. They are
also less able to make the essential connections, both within subjects and
across them, that impart order and foundation to teaching and learning.

colleges recognize students' active engagement in the learning process as a core value and practice, critical thinking will be mere rhetoric for academic discourses.

The critical thinking movement of the 1980s and 1990s produced a flurry of activity and literature, as well as many revised mission statements; yet whether it has fundamentally changed *how* we teach remains less clear. As Astleitner (2002) has observed, "Educational research activities showed that critical thinking is significantly anchored within curricula and related teaching goal taxonomies, but that it is not supported and taught systematically in daily instruction. The main reasons for this shortcoming are that teachers are not educated in critical thinking. . . . and that teachers have no time and other instructional resources to integrate critical thinking into their daily instruction" (p. 54). Thus there is a need for a comprehensive professional development model to help faculty learn how to teach for critical thinking.

## A Professional Development Model for Critical Thinking

In the early 1990s, the CCA faculty and I developed a learner-centered professional development model in order to implement the college's early critical thinking efforts. This model still holds promise for making the teaching—and learning—of critical thinking (as well as other teaching and learning practices) an even greater reality. The next section describes the essential components of this model.

**Find a Champion.** Any professional development effort for faculty needs a champion or champions to lead colleagues through the process of change. The champion's job is not to mandate, but to motivate; not to control, but to clarify; not to find fault, but to facilitate; not to talk too much, but to listen actively. This champion, most likely a faculty member, should be someone who has a passion for critical thinking, which may have been observed through classroom visitations, written publications, or conference or workshop presentations on the topic.

**Select Participants Wisely.** Selection of participants for any professional development project is important. Early adopters and others truly interested in working on a critical thinking project should participate in the project's ongoing professional development activities. Self-selection, recommendations (from the administration and students), and other means should be used to recruit energetic, interested faculty to participate.

**Involve Faculty in Planning.** Once a group of faculty have been selected or have volunteered to participate, they should plan the project themselves, because people tend to support what they help to create. Planning must involve contacting those who have already implemented and evaluated successful programs and should integrate information about others' successes and failures into project planning.

**Research Learning Experiences.** Various critical thinking models, materials, experts, and programs can form the basis for the professional development project. No one model or program meets all needs, so small teams of participants should research and recommend the kind of learning activities and experiences that will produce the results they want.

Information about successful initiatives already under way can be found in journals and magazines, at conferences, or through an Internet search. Project participants should correspond with those who have implemented successful programs in order to design a program that meets specific campus goals and objectives.

**Develop and Implement Curricula and Processes.** Once faculty have grappled with defining critical thinking, they should identify how it is to be taught (via the infusion model, which weaves critical thinking into an existing curriculum; the stand-alone course model; or the simultaneous course model, which pairs a critical thinking class with an existing course from another discipline).

Once faculty have defined how critical thinking is to be taught, participants then need to work together to develop appropriate curricula, determine processes for implementing these curricula, and facilitate sessions where faculty can practice using a variety of effective teaching and learning methods. After curricula have been developed and faculty have had the opportunity to practice how to teach their courses, professors are then ready to implement the teaching of and for critical thinking in their classroom.

**Implement Faculty Coaching.** Peer and other types of coaching play a critical role in implementing and sustaining institutional change. During the planning process, faculty should develop ways to coach each other through the change process. Effective methods include classroom observation and feedback; joint critique of videotaped teaching practice; paired, small-group, or whole-group meetings; electronic bulletin boards, chat rooms, or listservs; and so forth. Lasting instructional change requires a great deal of hand-holding; coaching is essential for project success.

**Ensure Institutional Support.** Institutional support for professional development efforts must be present if those efforts are to succeed. Whether by way of release time, additional pay, or use of meeting rooms and materials, participation of key administrators is necessary. Administrative support can take the form of press releases and newsletter articles, electronic or other bulletin boards highlighting project participants and activities, presentations made by key stakeholders at various functions, or hand-written thank-you notes to those involved. Participants in critical thinking professional development programs need tangible evidence that the institution supports and values their efforts. Trivial though it may seem, food and refreshments must be added to the menu of project activities.

**Assess Critical Thinking Practices.** Critical thinking efforts must be assessed to determine their effectiveness, and assessment tools and techniques should be selected or developed as part of the planning process. Rather than

**2**

*This chapter presents an overview of approaches to assessing critical thinking in community colleges, a brief description of standardized tests, and examples of several institutionally developed methodologies and good practices. Finally, it identifies challenges in assessing critical thinking in two-year colleges.*

# Assessing Critical Thinking in Community Colleges

*Trudy Bers*

Critical thinking is generally considered to be an important outcome of postsecondary education. Indeed, as Seybert (2002) notes, community colleges typically require degree-seeking students—and sometimes those pursuing a certificate—to take general education courses that include critical thinking. Rarely, however, do individual courses focus explicitly on critical thinking or carry the term in the course title. Rather, colleges often encourage or require courses in a variety of disciplines to incorporate critical thinking into learning objectives, or they may assume that across the range of courses a student takes to complete a degree she will have encountered assignments that foster and evaluate her ability to think critically.

As described in other chapters in this volume, there is a long-standing and unresolved controversy over whether critical thinking is best taught in courses focused specifically on it or in discipline-based courses in which it is explicitly or implicitly taught within the disciplinary framework and using discipline-specific subject matter.

Exacerbating the fact that colleges treat critical thinking differently in their curricula is the problem that it has no single accepted definition. Kurfiss (1988) asserts that three types of thinking interact in the critical thinking process: knowing the facts and concepts of the discipline, which he calls *declarative knowledge;* knowing how to reason, inquire, and present knowledge in the discipline, which he calls *procedural knowledge;* and being able to set goals, determine when additional information is needed, and assess the fruitfulness of a line of inquiry, which he calls *metacognition.*

Taylor (2004) presents a simpler definition of critical thinking employed at community colleges: "Critical thinking is the kind of thinking that professionals in the discipline use when doing the work of the discipline" (p. 2). Marzano, Pickering, and McTighe (1993) include critical thinking as a subset of abilities in the learning outcome they term "habits of mind." They describe critical thinking as a student's ability to be accurate and seek accuracy, be clear and seek clarity, be open-minded, restrain impulsivity, take a position when the situation warrants it, and be sensitive to the feelings and level of knowledge of others (as described in Huba and Freed, 2000).

Similarly, key elements of the definition proposed by Jones, Dougherty, Fantaske, and Hoffman (1997) are interpretation, analysis, evaluation, inference, presentation of argument, reflection, and disposition. Erwin and Sebrell (2003) assert that this definition is consensus-based, comprehensive, and useful because college and university faculty, employers, and policymakers all cited its components as among the skills college graduates should master.

## Assessing Critical Thinking

The multiple definitions of critical thinking, some of which are presented here, are mirrored by multiple approaches to assessing critical thinking. Though there is no one accepted approach (let alone one accepted assessment methodology or test), critical thinking assessment ought to simulate real-world problems that are messy, poorly defined, not soluble by rote knowledge or application of a structured rule, and lacking a single correct solution. Even standardized, closed-ended tests ought to exhibit these attributes.

**Characteristics of Critical Thinking Problems.** Huba and Freed (2000) describe the underlying principles and offer examples of techniques to assess critical thinking and problem-solving abilities. The educational goal for these assessments is to "learn to construct and defend reasonable solutions" (p. 203) to ill-defined problems that cannot be described with a high degree of completeness or certainty, and that cannot be solved in a way on which experts would necessarily agree. Huba and Freed present assessment examples from history, biology, mathematics, chemistry, psychology, and engineering.

Wiggins (1989) is another proponent of assessment approaches that require students to address problems analogous to those they will face in the real world. He characterizes such "true tests" as requiring performance of everyday tasks, replicating challenges and standards of performance faced by typical professionals in the field, and requiring human judgment and dialogue that is responsive to individual students.

**Characteristics of Measurable Behaviors.** Bloom (1956) identifies six levels of learning objectives: knowledge, comprehension, application, analysis, synthesis, and evaluation. At each level it is possible to assess measurable behavior, and because critical thinking takes place when students operate in the analysis, synthesis, and evaluation phases, Bloom's taxonomy

**Table 2.1.  Phases in Bloom's Taxonomy Relevant
to Critical Thinking**

| Phase | Behaviors |
|---|---|
| Analysis | Examine, classify, categorize, research, contrast, compare, disassemble, differentiate, separate, investigate, subdivide |
| Synthesis | Combine, hypothesize, construct, originate, create, design, formulate, role-play, develop |
| Evaluation | Compare, recommend, assess, value, apprise, solve, criticize, weigh, consider, debate |

can be considered an assessment of critical thinking. Behaviors for each level are shown in Table 2.1. Bloom's list of measurable behaviors can extend helpful guidance as institutions develop home-grown assessments of critical thinking.

**Characteristics of Exemplary Assessment Tasks.** Huba and Freed (2000) identify characteristics of exemplary assessment tasks. As an institution develops its own assessment or evaluates a standardized test, it may profit by determining to what extent each assessment or test exhibits these traits. Assessments are exemplary to the extent they are:

- Valid (they yield useful information to guide learning)
- Coherent (they lead to desired performance of product)
- Authentic (they address ill-defined problems or issues that are either emerging or enduring)
- Rigorous (they require use of declarative, procedural, and metacognitive knowledge)
- Engaging (they provoke student interest and persistence)
- Challenging (they encourage and evaluate student learning)
- Respectful (they allow students to reveal their uniqueness as learners)
- Responsive (they provide feedback to students leading to improvement) (Huba and Freed, 2000)

Exemplary assessments should also yield useful information to the institution to improve teaching and learning. They should be feasible to implement—taking into account both cost and administrative complexity—and should be intuitively understandable to faculty and other decision makers.

## Standardized Instruments

A number of standardized instruments that measure critical thinking are available. Additional information about each can be found on the test publisher's Website, and critiques and examples of the tests are offered in the assessment literature. Testing companies typically have a great deal of information about test validity and bias, as do articles focused specifically on these issues. Several publications contain a broad overview as well, notably Nichols and Nichols (2001), Borden and Owens (2001), and Erwin (1998). Here are the most well known and widely used standardized instruments for assessing critical thinking.

**Academic Profile.** This Educational Testing Service assessment examines college-level reading and critical thinking skills in the context of the humanities, social sciences, and natural sciences. The test is available in a standard form, which requires 120 minutes, or in an abbreviated form, requiring 40 minutes. Both criterion-referenced and norm-referenced scores are reported, which enables community colleges to determine whether students exhibit skills for each defined level of performance, and to compare their students over time or against students at other institutions.

**California Critical Thinking Dispositions Inventory (CCTDI).** This test, available from Insight Assessment (formerly the California Academic Press), targets students' internal motivation to use critical thinking skills to solve problems and make decisions. The seventy-five-item "agree-disagree" test measures the attributes of truth seeking, open-mindedness, analyticity, systematicity, inquisitiveness, confidence in reasoning, and cognitive maturity. The CCTDI is not a direct test of critical thinking, but its developers argue that if students do not have the inclination to use critical thinking skills they will not employ them in problem solving. Thus, they claim, the *disposition* to think critically is a key attribute to actually thinking critically.

**California Critical Thinking Skills Test (CCTST).** Also from Insight Assessment, the CCTST assesses an individual's or group's critical thinking and reasoning skills. It yields a total score and norm-group percentiles, as well as subscale scores by the classical categories of inductive and deductive reasoning and by the contemporary categories of analysis, inference, and evaluation.

**College BASE.** College BASE, developed at the University of Missouri-Columbia, is a criterion-referenced academic achievement test. Designed to be administered after students complete a college-level core curriculum, the test emphasizes concepts and principles from course materials. It tests knowledge and skills in English, mathematics, science, and social studies and gives performance rankings in higher-order thinking skills, such as interpretive, strategic, and adaptive reasoning abilities.

**Collegiate Assessment of Academic Proficiency (CAAP).** This ACT standardized test measures academic skills in five general education skill areas, among them critical thinking. According to CAAP literature, the test "measures the ability to clarify, analyze, evaluate, and extend arguments" (ACT, 2004, n.p.). Students read passages in a variety of formats (case study, dialogue, statistical argument, editorial) and answer multiple-choice questions for each passage. The CAAP can be used as an outcomes measure, as a measure of group change, as a cross-sectional or longitudinal study, or as a linkage vehicle to compare students' work on different though similar ACT tests (such as the ACT Assessment, ASSET, and COMPASS).

**Collegiate Learning Assessment Project (CLA).** The Rand Corporation's Council for Aid to Education has developed a new instrument to measure the value added by an institution to students' critical thinking skills (http://www.cae.org/content/pro_collegiate.htm). In this assessment, the institution is the unit of analysis. Students are given open-ended tasks and asked to write essays in response, which are then assessed for the ability to identify the strengths and limitations of an argument; present a coherent argument in support of a proposition; or interpret, analyze, and synthesize information. Students take the online test in a three-hour, proctored setting.

**Tasks in Critical Thinking.** Developed by the Educational Testing Service and the College Board, this test is performance-based and generates group rather than individual scores. Students are asked to solve a dilemma or task in an area of humanities, social sciences, and natural sciences. Scorers use rubrics to evaluate responses, targeting the skills areas of inquiry, analysis, and communication.

**Test of Everyday Reasoning.** This thirty-five-item multiple-choice test is produced by Insight Assessment and is designed to assess an individual's or group's basic reasoning skills. The test takes fifty minutes and yields a total score for overall reasoning skills, as well as three subscale scores in the categories of analysis, inference, and evaluation.

**Watson-Glaser Critical Thinking Appraisal.** This test was developed in the 1960s, and in addition to a total score it features five subscores in inference, recognition of assumption, deduction, interpretation, and evaluation of argument. This test, as with all of the standardized tests presented thus far, is intended to test students' ability to think critically.

Other standardized instruments permit less direct measure of these abilities either because national norms or standardized scores are not produced (as in the case of the Faciones' scoring rubric, to be described here) or because they rely on student self-reports of critical thinking competencies, gains, or behaviors thought to be associated with critical thinking. Although these tests are not direct measures of critical thinking, it is possible to draw inferences about critical thinking ability from these self-report assessments.

**Community College Survey of Student Engagement (CCSSE).** CCSSE, the community college counterpart to the National Survey of Student Engagement, contains a number of items asking students to report on the frequency with which they engage in various behaviors such as memorizing facts, ideas, or methods; analyzing the basic elements of an idea, experience, or theory; synthesizing and organizing ideas, information, or experiences; making judgments about the value or soundness of information, arguments, or methods; and applying theories or concepts to practical problems or in new situations. Available from the CCSSE office at the

University of Texas, Austin, the survey has been administered at more than two hundred community colleges. Data to construct national norms are becoming available, and studies are under way to link CCSSE results with other measures of critical thinking.

**Holistic Critical Thinking Scoring Rubric.** Facione and Facione (1994) developed a four-level scoring rubric to assess critical thinking and a set of instructions about how to use the rubric. It does not enable an institution to compare students' results with national norms, but it is based on extensive research on assessing critical thinking.

## Institutionally Developed Assessments

Several community colleges have each created an institution-specific methodology for assessing critical thinking. For example, Peter Dlugos (2003), at Bergen Community College in New Jersey, developed three assessment exercises that combine examination of students' personal growth and development with tests of their critical thinking ability. One exercise, "Living the Examined Life," focuses on changes a student would like to make in his life. The second, "Transforming Yourself into an Enlightened Being," deals with a student's definition of what it means to be "enlightened" and how she might transform herself to become enlightened. Dlugos's final exercise focuses on students' definition and practice of compassion. Rubrics enable an instructor to evaluate students' critical thinking, organizational, and writing skills even as they evaluate student growth and development. Dlugos's work is somewhat unusual because he concentrates on students' affective development as well as critical thinking in the same assessment.

Waukesha County Technical College in Wisconsin assesses twenty-three student learning outcomes under four Critical Life Skills Areas: communication skills, analytical skills (including critical thinking), group effectiveness skills, and personal management skills. In this assessment, critical thinking is defined as the ability to apply the techniques of analytical thinking and effective decision making. Six levels of competency are identified: defining common thinking strategies, identifying common thinking strategies within a personal or occupational setting, drawing logical conclusions from adequate evidence, examining reasons and evidence from different viewpoints, constructing a case in support of a claim, and assessing the validity of decisions and cases. Students' critical thinking skills are examined through an integrated assessment plan that includes course, department, and division evaluations. Students then receive a Critical Life Skills Transcript that identifies their level of achievement within each skill area.

The Community College of Baltimore County (Maryland) states that general education courses must teach critical analysis and reasoning by offering "a variety of learning experiences that encourage students, independently and in collaboration with others, to use those fundamental principles and methods to acquire, analyze, and use information for purposes of inquiry, critical thinking, problem-solving, and creative expression in a diverse environment" (Community College of Baltimore County, 2004, p. 2). The college uses a number of assessment approaches; the one most germane to assessing critical thinking is the GREAT project, initiated in 2001, which uses common graded assignments designed by teams of faculty from general education disciplines. Known as GREATs, the GeneRal Education Assessment Teams have developed a list of assignments and scoring rubrics for each discipline area, which are then incorporated into all sections of designated courses each semester. Trained faculty collect and score a random sample of these assignments at the end of the fall and spring semesters. On a 6-point scale, mean scores for the critical thinking rubric were 3.3 in fall 2003 and 3.8 in spring 2004. Scores indicated students were able to think critically to a moderate degree but were not outstanding. College staff assert that the GREAT project enables the institution to assess students' critical thinking learning outcomes and also permits professional development for faculty.

The College of DuPage (Illinois) has, for several years, administered six CAAP subject area tests each fall and spring to one hundred students. Students are chosen by randomly selecting classes, and instructors have been generally willing to allocate class time for their students to take the CAAP. The results are analyzed, and differentiation is made among entering freshmen, students midway through their associate degree, and those completing their sophomore year.

One interesting finding from the first two years of the CAAP is that students' critical thinking skills are dependent on reading ability (College of DuPage, 2000). From this finding, the college initiated a pilot project asking students to respond to a specific question according to their reading of two brief opposing essays on a topic (for example, "Does recycling make economic sense?"). The college is currently reviewing data from this pilot.

For the pilot study, a specific rubric was developed by an interdisciplinary faculty task force. The skills targeted in this design include communication of ideas, information literacy skills, synthesis and critical thinking skills, and ways of thinking and knowing. Entry-level students are compared with exit-level students in blind scoring. The rubric has been shown to be sensitive enough to demonstrate an increased skill-set across the dimensions measured (Russ Watson, personal communication, July 2004).

Perry (2004) studied critical thinking in Web-based community college courses in Maryland. He examined thirty-eight Websites for courses taught in spring 2004 and identified eight types of assignments that could be used to assess critical thinking: open-ended real-world examples, weekly assignments, discussion boards, multiple-choice tests, essay tests, journals, formal papers, and speeches. Almost all assignments (99 percent) were individual rather than group and were evenly divided between direct and indirect assessments of critical thinking. At Harold Washington College in Chicago, the faculty assessment committee undertook a multipart critical thinking assessment project beginning in 2003. The committee first defined critical thinking, and committee members went back to colleagues in their departments several times for feedback until a consensus-based definition emerged. The committee then developed learning outcomes based on the definition, again seeking feedback from departments.

Third, the committee reviewed existing critical thinking tests to identify one that could be administered within a standard class meeting time, was consistent with learning outcomes, and had utility for faculty who took the test themselves. The college finally selected the California Critical Thinking Skills Test, and in fall 2003 roughly sixteen hundred students took the test and supplied demographic information. Results showed that students scored below the national sample of two-year college students, but not significantly so. As a result, the assessment committee is presenting a series of workshops on critical thinking strategies to train faculty to embed critical thinking activities (general and discipline-specific) into their classrooms and curricula. The college will administer the CCTST again in fall 2005 to assess progress (Cecilia Lopez, personal communication, July 2004).

Metropolitan Community College (Missouri) faculty have administered the Watson-Glaser test for five years. Recent analyses of more than two thousand test results showed that students did not score as well as desired on the subtest pertaining to inference. As a result, faculty developed course-embedded assignments focusing on inference and a scoring rubric. In 2003, the assignments were embedded in American history courses, and in fall 2004 a modified instrument was extended to psychology, sociology, political science, and criminal justice courses (Charles Van Middlesworth, personal communication, March 2005).

## Challenges in Assessing Critical Thinking

Assessing community college students' critical thinking presents many challenges and issues. Some issues are similar to those inherent in constructing and implementing any assessment of student learning outcomes: test validity and reliability, students taking seriously an exercise that may not count in their course grade or graduation requirements, funding for standardized tests or institutional projects, and helping faculty understand the need to assess student learning outcomes to meet both institutional and external expectations.

These challenges are particularly germane to community colleges, but many of them are relevant to virtually any commuter, nonselective postsecondary institution that enrolls a large number of part-time adult students whose enrollment patterns are often characterized by stop-outs, swirling among multiple schools, or discontinuous enrollment over an extended period of time.

In addition, because so many community college students are older, have significant work experience, and are raising their own families, they have probably already encountered many situations in which critical thinking was essential—which calls into question the relative impact of community college critical thinking programs. Yet the argument can be made that how and where a student acquires critical thinking skills is not important; what is important is that a student has them, especially after completing a stipulated amount of college work, or a course specifically targeted to critical thinking.

A key issue for assessment is timing, because many community college students do not persist through an official degree. In fact, students' departure is usually noted after the fact (when they do not return), and students frequently create their own curricula to meet what they perceive to be career, transfer, or personal objectives. Thus it is nearly impossible to capture students at a catalogue-defined terminal point in their program. As well, it may be difficult to assess critical thinking outside the classroom. Recently, a number of community colleges in Illinois participated in a Pew-funded initiative to assess student learning by taking sections of the ACT WorkKeys and the Community College Survey of Student Engagement. Each college, given $1,000 to offset implementation costs, created its own incentive system for encouraging students to participate. Colleges indicated it was often difficult to obtain student cooperation to take the tests even when incentives such as cash and gift certificates were available.

Finally, although the literature is virtually unanimous in asserting that strong support from the president or academic vice president is essential for a successful assessment program, the need for a champion who actually organizes the details and does the work is rarely highlighted. Yet a survey of critical thinking programs on community college Websites demonstrated that without such a champion to lead the assessment project—not just verbally or as a figurehead, but by doing the details year after year—programs may wither or fade away.

## Conclusion

Several conclusions regarding the assessment of critical thinking in community colleges have emerged from the research conducted for this chapter. One is that colleges continue to assert that critical thinking is a crucial skill they want and expect their students to possess upon completion of their college experience. A second is that assessment of critical thinking is far more likely to take place at the course level, usually with an instructor assessing his or her own students, than at the department, program, or institutional level. A third and related conclusion is that community colleges are still, for the most part, in the planning stage for conducting assessment of critical thinking at the program or institutional level. Many colleges noted they have or are creating rubrics to use in evaluating student work, but few came forward with a description of a completed project that uses rubrics for assessing critical thinking, and even fewer had results available or information about how the results were used to revise programs and courses, improve student learning, or refine the assessment process itself. The GREAT project at the Community College of Baltimore County is one exception.

However success is defined, which itself is a topic meriting substantial discussion, the pressure for community colleges to be accountable, present evidence that students are successful, and offer students crucial learning and life skills will continue. The assessment movement is well into its second decade, yet colleges as a group have made little measurable progress in assessing students' critical thinking abilities and learning outcomes beyond the individual class level, despite the fact that critical thinking is a primary learning objective in many institutions.

### References

ACT. *College Assessment of Academic Proficiency, CAAP: Assessing Academic Achievement in Reading, Writing, Mathematics, Science, and Critical Thinking.* Iowa City, Iowa: ACT, 2004.

Bloom, B. (ed.). *A Taxonomy of Educational Objectives. Handbook I: Cognitive Domain.* New York: McKay, 1956.

Borden, V.M.H., and Owens, J.L.Z. *Measuring Quality: Choosing Among Surveys and Other Assessments of College Quality.* Washington, D.C.: American Council on Education, 2001.

College of DuPage. "General Education Skills Development: An Analysis of Students' General Educational Skills Development at College of DuPage Utilizing Four Rounds of CAAP Scores—Fall 1998, 1999 to Spring 1999, 2000." Glen Ellyn, Ill.: College of DuPage, 2000. http://www.cod.edu/Dept/Outcomes/SOAGnEd/CP00Rpt.pdf. Accessed Feb. 8, 2005.

Community College of Baltimore County. "Progress Reports on Student Learning Outcomes Assessment." Baltimore, Md.: Community College of Baltimore County, 2004.

Dlugos, P. "Using Critical Thinking to Assess the Ineffable." *Community College Journal of Research and Practice,* 2003, 27, 613–629.

Erwin, T. D. *The NPEC Sourcebook on Assessment.* Vol. 1: *Definitions and Assessment Methods for Critical Thinking, Problem Solving, and Writing.* Washington, D.C.: National Center for Education Statistics, U.S. Department of Education, 1998.

Erwin, T. D., and Sebrell, K. W. "Assessment of Critical Thinking: ETS's Tasks in Critical Thinking." *Journal of General Education,* 2003, 52(1), 50–70.

Facione, P. A., and Facione, N. C. *Holistic Critical Thinking Scoring Rubric.* Millbrae: California Academic Press, 1994. http://www.insightassessment.com/HCTSR.html. Accessed Feb. 8, 2004.

Huba, M. E., and Freed, J. E. *Learner-Centered Assessment on College Campuses: Shifting the Focus from Teaching to Learning.* Boston: Allyn and Bacon, 2000.

Jones, E. A., Dougherty, B. C., Fantaske, P., and Hoffman, S. *Identifying College Graduates' Essential Skills in Reading and Problem Solving: Perspectives of Faculty, Employers and Policymakers.* University Park, Pa.: U.S. Department of Education, 1997.

Kurfiss, J. G. *Critical Thinking: Theory, Research, Practice, and Possibilities.* ASHE-ERIC Higher Education Report no. 2. College Station, Tex.: Association for the Study of Higher Education, 1988.

Marzano, R. J., Pickering, D., and McTighe, J. *Assessing Student Outcomes: Performance Assessment Using the Dimensions of Learning Model.* Alexandria, Va.: Association for Supervision and Curriculum Development, 1993.

Nichols, J. O., and Nichols, K. W. *General Education Assessment for Improvement of Student Academic Achievement: Guidance for Academic Departments and Committees.* New York: Agathon Press, 2001.

Perry, G. E. "Critical Thinking and Web-Based Education in Maryland Community Colleges: How the Medium Promotes Development." Unpublished doctoral dissertation, University of West Virginia, 2004.

Seybert, J. "Assessing Student Learning Outcomes." In T. H. Bers and H. Calhoun (eds.), *Next Steps for the Community College.* New Directions for Community Colleges, no. 117. San Francisco: Jossey-Bass, 2002.

Taylor, B. "Debating Moral Education—Topic 3: Teaching and Learning." Paper presented at Center for Academic Integrity conference, Duke University, July 2004.

Wiggins, G. "A True Test: Toward More Authentic and Equitable Assessment." *Phi Delta Kappan,* May 1989, 703–713.

*TRUDY BERS is executive director of research, curriculum, and planning at Oakton Community College in Des Plaines, Illinois.*

The goal of this chapter is to explicate the depth of this problem and detail its solution: a comprehensive, substantive concept of critical thinking fostered across the curriculum. We must not rest content with a fuzzy or overly narrow concept of critical thinking. We need a rich, substantive concept with clear-cut implications for ensuring that students construct knowledge and then transfer it to the multiple facets of their lives. Only a substantive concept of critical thinking affords the durability, flexibility, and richness of detail essential for planning long-term professional development to serve that end.

## Foundations for a Substantive Concept of Critical Thinking

Let us begin with the foundations. The idea of critical thinking, stripped to its essentials, can be expressed in a number of ways. Here's one: critical thinking is the art of thinking about thinking in an intellectually disciplined manner. Critical thinkers explicitly focus on thinking in three interrelated phases. They *analyze* thinking, they *assess* thinking, and they *improve* thinking (as a result). *Creative thinking* is the work of the third phase, the phase of replacing weak thinking with strong thinking, or of replacing strong thinking with stronger thinking. Creative thinking, from this vantage point, is a natural by-product of critical thinking, precisely because analyzing and assessing thinking enables one to raise it to a higher level—to recreate it, as it were. New and better thinking is the by-product of healthy critical thought (Paul and Elder, 2004b).

A person is a critical thinker to the extent that he or she regularly improves thinking by studying and *critiquing* it. Critical thinkers painstakingly study how humans can better ground, develop, and apply thought. The basic idea is simple: study thinking for strengths and weaknesses. Then improve it as a result. A critical thinker does not say: "My thinking is pretty good on the whole. I don't really need to think much about it; I just need to use it intuitively." A critical thinker says: "My thinking, and that of most people, is often flawed. The flaws that exist commonly in thinking frequently lead to significant problems in human life. It is foolish ever to take thinking for granted. If we want to think well, we must regularly analyze, assess, and reconstruct it."

In the remainder of this chapter, I spell out the multiple ways in which a robust concept of critical thinking—grounded in the concept I have briefly sketched—enables one to make essential connections that integrate these foundational insights into teaching and learning. I also document the fact that few faculty today have a robust concept of critical thinking. Of necessity, the connections to which I allude are not fully explained in this short chapter. Interested readers should consult http://www.criticalthinking.org for articles detailing these connections.

## Essential Connections Between a Substantive Concept and Teaching and Learning

The concept of critical thinking, rightly understood, ties together much of what we, as teachers and learners, need to understand, and it enables us to foster institutional change. Let us look at some of the important connections faculty and administrators begin to make as they internalize a substantive concept of critical thinking.

**A Natural Marriage Exists Between Academic Disciplines and Critical Thinking.** A discipline is not a collection of isolated and assorted facts (despite the fact that it is often taught as such). Rather, it is a system of interrelated meanings with definitive logic that presupposes and uses critical thinking concepts and tools (Elder and Paul, 2003; Paul and Elder, 2004a). Biology, for example, is critical thinking applied to living systems. History is critical thinking applied to events and patterns in the past. Sociology is critical thinking applied to the study of human groups and group behavior. Each discipline generates a *form of thinking*. Biology generates biological thinking; history, historical thinking; sociology, sociological thinking. Each (disciplined) form of thinking is a contextualization of critical thinking. When inquiry (in any discipline) is not based on sound critical thinking, it often results in error, misunderstanding, myth, or illusion.

**A Natural Relationship Exists Between Becoming a Skilled Thinker and Becoming a Skilled Learner.** It makes no sense to say, "I'm not a very good thinker, but I am an effective learner." If becoming a good thinker requires that we learn to regularly think about our thinking, becoming a skilled learner requires that we learn to regularly think about our learning. The skills in upgrading thinking are the same skills as those required in upgrading learning. For example, to be a skilled thinker requires that we regularly make explicit the fundamental structures that underlie all thinking and learning: What is my purpose? What question am I trying to answer? What data or information do I need? What conclusions or inferences can I make (that are based on this information)? If I come to these conclusions, what are the implications and consequences? What is the key concept (theory, principle, axiom) I am working with? What assumptions am I making? What is my point of view? (See Figure 3.1.)

Of course, it is not enough to take our thinking and learning apart through analysis; we must also evaluate both to determine their quality. We must internalize fundamental intellectual standards that are indispensable to the quality of thinking and learning. This means that as thinkers and learners we must develop the ability to assess thinking for its clarity and accuracy, for its precision and relevance, for its depth and breadth, and for its logic and significance (Figure 3.2).

**A Substantive Concept of Critical Thinking Addresses the Need for Deep Learning.** Teaching based on a substantive concept of critical thinking

## Figure 3.1.  Elements of Thought

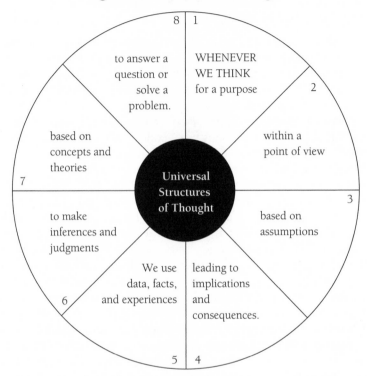

appeals to reason and evidence. It encourages students to discover as well as process information. It provides occasions in which students think their way to conclusions; defend positions on difficult issues; consider a variety of points of view; analyze concepts, theories, and explanations; clarify issues and conclusions; solve problems; transfer ideas to new contexts; examine assumptions; assess alleged facts; explore implications and consequences; and increasingly come to terms with the contradictions and inconsistencies of their own thought and experience. It engages students in forms of thinking that enable them to deeply master content.

**A Substantive Concept of Critical Thinking Leads to Teaching for Acquisition of Substantive Knowledge.** Substantive knowledge is a special form of knowledge that is foundational, significant, and useful. It is knowledge that leads to further knowledge and to vital questions (that, in turn, lead to further knowledge and more vital questions, and so on; Elder and Paul, 2002). Acquiring substantive knowledge is equivalent to acquiring effective organizers for the mind that enable us to weave everything we learn into a tapestry, a system, an integrated whole. Substantive knowledge is found in the set of fundamental concepts and principles that lie at the

## Figure 3.2.  Intellectual Standards

| | |
|---|---|
| Clarity | Could you elaborate?<br>Could you give me an example?<br>Could you illustrate what you mean? |
| Accuracy | How could we check on that?<br>How could we find out if that is true?<br>How could we verify or test that? |
| Precision | Could you be more specific?<br>Could you give me more details?<br>Could you be more exact? |
| Relevance | How does that relate to the problem?<br>How does that bear on the question?<br>How does that help us with the issue? |
| Depth | What factors make this a difficult problem?<br>What are some of the complexities of this question?<br>What are some of the difficulties we need to deal with? |
| Breadth | Do we need to look at this from another perspective?<br>Do we need to consider another point of view?<br>Do we need to look at this in others ways? |
| Logic | Does all this make sense together?<br>Does your first paragraph fit in with your last?<br>Does what you say follow from the evidence? |
| Significance | Is this the most important problem to consider?<br>Is this the central idea to focus on?<br>Which of these facts are most important? |
| Fairness | Do I have any vested interest in this issue?<br>Am I sympathetically representing the viewpoints of others? |

heart of understanding everything in a discipline or subject. For example, if you understand deeply what a biological cell is and the five essential characteristics of all living systems, if you understand how healthy cells function and how unhealthy cells alter that functioning, and if you begin to study how cells become dysfunctional, you have the substantive knowledge that leads you to ask vital questions about living things. You begin to *think biologically*.

Every discipline and every subject contains crucial information students need if they are to acquire substantive knowledge in that subject. The basic tools of critical thinking are the essential tools for acquiring this knowledge. They enable students to acquire a rich and extensive knowledge of content, and they simultaneously furnish the means for knowledge to become a *permanent acquisition* in the mind.

**A Natural Relationship Exists Between Critical Thinking and Skilled Reading and Writing.** The reflective mind improves its thinking by reflectively thinking about it. Likewise, it improves its reading by reflectively thinking about what (and how) it reads (Paul and Elder, 2003b) and improves its writing by analyzing and assessing each draft it creates (Paul and Elder, 2003c). It moves back and forth between the cognitive (thinking) and the meta-cognitive (thinking about thinking). It moves forward a bit and then loops back on itself to assess its own operations. It checks its tracks. It makes good its ground. It rises above itself and exercises oversight on itself.

One of the most important abilities a thinker can have is the ability to monitor and assess his or her own thinking while processing the thinking of others. In reading, for example, the reflective mind monitors how it is reading while it is reading. The foundation for this ability is knowledge of how the mind functions when reading well. For example, if I know that to read for deep understanding I must actively bring ideas taken from a written text into my thinking, I intentionally paraphrase as I read. I put the meaning of each key sentence I read into my own words. If I know that one can understand ideas best when they are exemplified, then as a writer I give my readers intuitive examples of what I am saying. In a parallel way, as a reader I look for examples to better understand what a text is saying. Learning how to read closely and write substantively presuppose critical thinking abilities. When I read closely, I take ownership of important ideas in a text. When I write substantively, I say something worth saying about a subject of importance. When we understand, as instructors, what it takes to read closely and write substantively—that students must *think their way through* what they read and what they write—then we design instruction that explicitly links thinking with reading and writing.

## Further Implications of a Robust Concept of Critical Thinking

With a substantive concept of critical thinking deeply rooted in our thinking:

- We can explain critical thinking clearly to our students
- We use it to give order and meaning to our teaching and to our students' learning
- We use it as a central organizer in the design of instruction
- We understand the integral relationship between thinking and content
- We teach content as we foster thinking, and we teach thinking as the key to understanding content
- We model the thinking students must do to take ownership of content
- We conceptualize students as thinkers who must actively think their way through content if they are to internalize it
- We recognize and teach the intellectual traits—dispositions essential to thinking well—within the disciplines (Figure 3.3)

In short, once we understand critical thinking substantively, we can teach students to use critical thinking "tools" to enter into any system of

**Figure 3.3. Intellectual Traits**

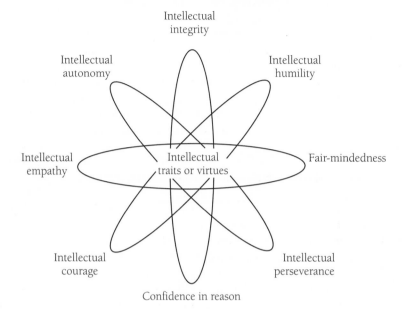

Intellectual
integrity

Intellectual
autonomy

Intellectual
humility

Intellectual
empathy

Intellectual
traits or virtues

Fair-mindedness

Intellectual
courage

Intellectual
perseverance

Confidence in reason

thought and think within it. With this understanding, we naturally abandon a didactic style of teaching, because we recognize its ineffectiveness.
We focus more energy on helping students construct, in their own mind,
the concepts that define the various disciplines they are studying. With a
substantive concept of critical thinking at the heart of our thinking, we
begin to collect and experiment with an array of classroom teaching strategies that foster students' mastery of content and development of disciplined
reasoning (Paul and Elder, 2003a).

## Most Faculty Lack a Substantive Concept of Critical Thinking

Despite the integral relationship between critical thinking and the con-
struction of knowledge, studies show that most college faculty lack a substantive concept of critical thinking (Paul, Elder, and Bartell, 1997).
Consequently, critical thinking is rarely used as a central organizer in
designing instruction. It does not inform most faculty members' conception
of the student's role as learner. It does not affect how faculty conceptualize
their own role as instructors. Faculty often fail to link critical thinking to
the essential thinking that defines the content they teach. Therefore they
usually teach content as separate from the thinking students must do if they
are to take ownership of that content. They teach history but not *historical
thinking*. They teach biology, but not *biological thinking*. They teach math,

but not *mathematical thinking.* They expect students to engage in analysis but have no clear idea of the *elements* of analysis (or how to teach students those elements). They want students to use intellectual standards in their thinking but have no clear conception of what intellectual standards they want their students to use or how to articulate them. They are unable to describe the intellectual traits (dispositions) essential to the educated mind. They have no clear idea of the relation of critical thinking to creative thinking, nor to problem solving, decision making, or communication. They are not sure how to deeply connect critical thinking concepts to the concepts within their discipline. They use a didactic style of teaching that is ineffective and fails to foster students' ability to internalize basic concepts within disciplines. They lack classroom teaching strategies that would foster students' ability to master content and become skilled learners.

Faculty have these problems. Yet they don't, as a rule, know that they have them. The majority of college faculty consider their teaching strategies to be quite effective, despite significant evidence to the contrary (Gardiner, 1995). They see whatever problems exist in the learning process as the fault of students or beyond their control. Consider results from a large study (Paul, Elder, and Bartell, 1997) of faculty randomly selected from thirty-eight public and twenty-eight private colleges and universities. The study focused on the question, "To what extent are faculty teaching for critical thinking?" In forty-to-fifty-minute interviews, faculty were asked both closed- and open-ended questions about their understanding of critical thinking and how they teach for it (if at all). In the open-ended part of the interview, most faculty could give only a vague response. Much internal "tension" was apparent in their answers, and in some cases outright contradiction. Many reduced critical thinking to such phrases as "constructivism," "Bloom's taxonomy," "process-based," "inquiry-based," "beyond recall," "active learning," or "meaning-centered"—phrases that, under probing questions, the majority of faculty were unable to explain in relation to critical thinking. The most common confusion, perhaps, was between what is necessary for critical thinking and what is merely sufficient. For example, active engagement is necessary to critical thinking, but one can be actively engaged and not think critically.

By direct statement or by implication, most faculty claimed that they permeated their instruction with an emphasis on critical thinking and that the students internalized the concepts in their courses as a result. Yet only the rare interviewee mentioned the importance of students thinking clearly, accurately, precisely, relevantly, or logically. Very few mentioned any of the basic skills of thought such as the ability to clarify questions, gather relevant data, reason to logical or valid conclusions, identify key assumptions, trace significant implications, or enter without distortion into alternative points of view. Faculty in the study rarely mentioned intellectual traits of mind, such as intellectual humility, intellectual perseverance, or intellectual responsibility (Paul, Elder, and Bartell, 1997).

In addition, although the overwhelming majority (89 percent) of faculty claimed critical thinking to be a primary objective of their instruction, only a small minority (19 percent) could give a clear explanation of what critical thinking is. Furthermore, given their answers, only 9 percent of the respondents were clearly teaching for critical thinking on a typical day in class.

Although a great majority (78 percent) of faculty claimed their students lacked appropriate intellectual standards to use in assessing their thinking, and 73 percent considered students' learning to assess their own work to be of primary importance, only a very small minority (8 percent) could enumerate any intellectual criteria or standards they required of students or could give an intelligible explanation of what those criteria and standards were.

Although 50 percent of those interviewed said they explicitly distinguished critical thinking skills from traits, only 8 percent were able to offer a clear conception of the critical thinking skills they thought most important for their students to develop. Furthermore, the majority alluded either minimally or vaguely (33 percent) or not at all (42 percent) to intellectual traits of mind.

Similarly, although two-thirds (67 percent) of faculty interviewed for this study said that their concept of critical thinking is largely explicit in their thinking, only 19 percent could elaborate on their concept. As well, though the great majority (89 percent) stated that critical thinking was of primary importance to their instruction, 77 percent of respondents had little, limited, or no conception of how to reconcile content coverage with the fostering of critical thinking.

The overwhelming majority (81 percent) felt that their department's graduates develop a good or high level of critical thinking ability while in their program. Yet only 20 percent said their department had a shared approach to critical thinking, and only 9 percent were able to clearly articulate how they would assess the extent to which a faculty member was or was not fostering critical thinking. The remaining respondents had a limited conception, or none at all, of how to do this (Paul, Elder, and Bartell, 1997). This study reveals a great deal about how little typical faculty members know about critical thinking, and yet—in contrast—how much they think they know.

## Overcoming Conceptual Obstacles

We cannot get beyond nonsubstantive concepts of critical thinking unless we face the obstacles to them and devise effective countermeasures. For example, research proves—and common sense recognizes—that it is largely ineffective to attempt to "give" students knowledge through traditional "high coverage" didactic lectures. Yet traditional lecture-centered pedagogy continues to dominate instruction, as if one could acquire knowledge simply by listening to a lecture and memorizing its components and details. As a result, students often develop the skill of short-term memorization and use it to get high grades. Many faculty uncritically assume that students are doing more than developing their short-term memory, but at the same time many recognize that students often forget most of what they memorize from semester to semester, and they would also admit that students on the whole are not developing the ability to think within the subject of their degree.

Few faculty recognize what it takes to transform instruction so that students routinely use their thinking to take ownership of course content. Few faculty know or use learning strategies that enable students to think analytically through content. Few understand critical thinking as a set of tools for acquiring knowledge. Few understand what it means to teach content as thinking.

At the same time, faculty and administrators often mistakenly think critical thinking skills and abilities can be effectively taught in one or two specific courses tailor-made to teach these skills and abilities. Sometimes this mistaken view takes the form of advocating for a general education course in critical thinking or for stand-alone study skills courses. Such courses can, of course, make some contribution to student learning, but we should not delude ourselves into thinking that one or two courses can effectively substitute for an organized emphasis on critical thinking across the curriculum, within every subject and discipline, and across a number of years. Failure to recognize the limitations of such stand-alone courses is a serious obstacle to the reform of instruction. We can better understand this by analyzing the thinking that underlies the adoption of such courses.

**Establishing General Education Courses in Critical Thinking Does Not Solve the Problem.** There are a number of reasons establishing general education courses in critical thinking does not, by itself, foster critical thinking within academic disciplines. The first is that the majority of such courses are based in a particular discipline (such as philosophy or English) and typically teach only the aspects of critical thinking traditionally highlighted within those disciplines. For example, critical thinking courses taught in philosophy departments most likely substitute either formal or informal logic for critical thinking. Such a course taught in an English department probably focuses on persuasive writing and rhetoric. Though perhaps valuable in themselves, none of these emphases comes close to capturing a substantive concept of critical thinking. As a result, instructors in other departments fail to see the relevance of what students are taught in critical thinking courses to their discipline (for example, an English instructor might ask how formal logic can help students in her poetry class). Therefore these courses are ignored by the faculty at large. In turn, the courses do little to help students become skilled learners.

**Establishing General Education Courses in Study Skills Does Not Solve the Problem.** Just as a general education course in critical thinking does not suffice to foster skilled and disciplined reasoning across the curriculum, study skills courses alone do not solve the problem. This is true, in part, because most study skills courses are not based on a substantive concept of critical thinking. Indeed, most lack *any* unifying theory or organizing concept. For example, they do not typically teach students how to analyze thinking using the elements of thought. They do not typically teach students intellectual standards, nor how to assess their own work using these standards. They do not teach students how to begin to think within a discipline. Finally, because what is learned is intellectually fragmented, the content of such courses is typically soon forgotten. What is often missing is the coherence, connection, and depth of understanding that accompanies systematic critical thinking.

## Making Long-Term Plans

There are certain necessary conditions for successfully implementing a substantive concept of critical thinking: a long-term plan for institutional improvement; links to accreditation, mission statement, and outcomes assessment; a new emphasis on engaging students to think critically and deeply through course content; and a robust concept of critical thinking applied across the curriculum.

Short-term reform can do no more than foster surface reform. Deep change takes time, patience, perseverance, understanding, and commitment. This is not easy in an educational world saturated with glossy, superficial, quick fixes, a world historically plagued by a very short attention span. Nevertheless, a well-devised long-term professional development program, focused on progressive improvement of instruction through developing the critical thought of teachers, promises the long-term payoffs that make in-depth reform cost-effective.

But only when those designing professional development programs have a substantive concept of critical thinking will they have the requisite comprehensive insights that enable them to tie all professional development together and place substantive critical thinking squarely at the heart of it. Only then can they convince faculty of the need for a long-term approach. Only then will faculty be able to develop meaningful examples of critical thinking across the disciplines and discuss intellectual standards or the basic elements of thought. Only then can they make the connection of critical thinking to close reading or substantive writing. Only then will they be able to explain why cooperative learning, however necessary, is not enough. Only then can they explain the integral relationship between content and thinking, and begin to foster this understanding within their discipline.

## References

Elder, L., and Paul, R. *The Miniature Guide to the Art of Asking Essential Questions.* Dillon Beach, Calif.: Foundation for Critical Thinking, 2002.

Elder, L., and Paul, R. *A Miniature Guide to the Foundations of Analytic Thinking.* Dillon Beach, Calif.: Foundation for Critical Thinking, 2003.

Gardiner, L. *Redesigning Higher Education: Producing Dramatic Gains in Student Learning* (ASHE-ERIC Higher Education Report, vol. 23, no. 7). Washington, D.C.: Graduate School of Education and Human Development, George Washington University, 1995.

Paul, R., and Elder, L. *A Miniature Guide for Those Who Teach on How to Improve Student Learning: 30 Practical Ideas.* Dillon Beach, Calif.: Foundation for Critical Thinking, 2003a.

Paul, R., and Elder, L. *The Thinkers Guide to How to Read a Paragraph and Beyond: The Art of Close Reading.* Dillon Beach, Calif.: Foundation for Critical Thinking, 2003b.

Paul, R., and Elder, L. *The Thinkers Guide to How to Write a Paragraph: The Art of Substantive Writing.* Dillon Beach, Calif.: Foundation for Critical Thinking, 2003c.

Paul, R., and Elder, L. *The Miniature Guide to Critical Thinking Concepts and Tools.* Dillon Beach, Calif.: Foundation for Critical Thinking, 2004a.

Paul, R., and Elder, L. *The Thinkers Guide to the Nature and Functions of Critical and Creative Thought.* Dillon Beach, Calif.: Foundation for Critical Thinking, 2004b.

Paul, R., Elder, L., and Bartell, T. *California Teacher Preparation for Instruction in Critical Thinking: Research Findings and Policy Recommendations.* Sacramento: California Commission on Teacher Credentialing, 1997.

RICHARD PAUL *is director of research and professional development at the Center for Critical Thinking in Dillon Beach, California, and chair of the National Council for Excellence in Critical Thinking.*

*Critical thinking is foundational to the effective teaching of any subject, and it must be at the heart of any professional development program. This chapter presents a long-term professional development model based on a substantive concept of critical thinking, and ties critical thinking to the concept of the Learning College.*

# Critical Thinking as the Key to the Learning College: A Professional Development Model

*Linda Elder*

In Chapter Three, Richard Paul details a substantive concept of critical thinking. With this concept clearly in mind, we realize that substantive critical thinking should be the guiding force for all our educational efforts. We begin to see the pressing need for a staff development program that fosters critical thinking within and across the curriculum. Critical thinking, rightly understood, is not one of many possible "angles" for professional development. Rather, it should be the guiding force behind any and all professional development. This chapter outlines the key components of a professional development model based on critical thinking, and describes how one community college has tied critical thinking to the concept of the Learning College.

## Key Components of a Professional Development Program Based on Critical Thinking

Throughout its twenty-five years of existence, the Center for Critical Thinking has designed critical thinking staff development programs and workshops for more than sixty thousand college faculty from the United States and abroad. In this section, using the insights gained throughout these twenty-five years, I lay out essential components of any effective professional development program that is to be based on critical thinking.

**Identify the Gap Between the Ideal and the Real.** In designing a practical professional development program, we should first articulate what is entailed in the *ideal* college and then compare this ideal to actual practice

New Directions for Community Colleges, no. 130, Summer 2005 © Wiley Periodicals, Inc.

on our own campuses. Until we clearly have in mind what the ideal learning college would look like, we can't hope to achieve it. Thus it is important to begin with a set of questions:

- What is an educated person?
- What are the skills and abilities of educated people?
- What are the dispositions of educated people?
- What are educated people able to do in their thinking that uneducated persons cannot (or do not)?
- What is an ideal college, an ideal learning environment?
- What intellectual skills, abilities, and traits would we like to see all of our graduates have when they leave the college?

Having thought through these questions, we then need to assess how far our college is from the ideal. Specifically, we need to determine:

- What are the standard teaching practices at the college?
- How do these practices aid or hinder intellectual development?
- How can we bridge the gap between what we would ideally like to see happen and what is actually happening?
- What political realities affect the college's ability to place thinking at the center of teaching?
- How can we best take these realities into account?
- What skills needed to foster critical thinking do our faculty now lack?

**Foster a Critical Thinking Climate.** It is entirely possible that one, or two, or even a handful of faculty at a given college are fostering critical thinking. But this is not enough to promote disciplined reasoning across the student body. At the outset of any professional development program, we need to determine how we can best foster a college climate focused on developing thinking abilities. We cannot force faculty to place thinking at the center of teaching. But we can create an atmosphere that places thinking at the focal point of the college's philosophy, mission, and goals. We can provide support and even incentives for faculty to learn the foundations of critical thinking, so that they can begin to integrate it into their teaching. We can also tie assessment of faculty and the college as a whole to the fostering of critical thinking. These are necessary conditions if thinking is to play a primary role in learning across the campus.

**Understand the Importance of Administrative Commitment to Critical Thinking.** Creating a college climate that places critical thinking at the heart of teaching requires not only administrative support but also administrative commitment. Initially, this commitment might come from only one or two key administrators. But the commitment must be based on a substantive concept of critical thinking, and it must become deep and lasting in the mind of the lead administrator(s). As Paul has said, "critical thinking is not something to be devoured in a single sitting nor yet in a couple of workshops. It is to be savored and reflected upon. It is something to live and grow with, over years, over a lifetime" (2004, p. 1).

Unfortunately, few administrators demonstrate a deep interest in critical thinking. Yet to become effective instructional leaders, administrators must work their way slowly and methodically through the theory of critical thinking and apply it in their work and their lives. Only then do they see it as the heart of teaching and learning. Only then can they begin to persuade others to take a similar interest.

Although at least one administrator committed to critical thinking is a necessary condition for effective professional development, it is not sufficient. A professional development program cannot, in the long run, be dependent on one person. In the end, critical thinking must become the defining concept for the college.

**Establish an Advisory Team to Guide the Process.** In addition to at least one key administrator, a leadership team of administrators and faculty must be established to guide the reform process. This team must be in a position to positively influence faculty and staff across the campus.

**Take a Long-Term Approach.** A professional development program can succeed only through a long-term approach. A commitment to critical thinking is a commitment to continuous improvement; it is not something you do once and then are done with. Having said this, I will add that the initial stages involve a more intense focus, particularly in providing resources and supporting faculty as they develop their understanding of critical thinking. This initial process entails five to seven years of workshops and consultation with experts in fostering critical thinking across the curriculum.

A long-term approach is not possible if the program is vulnerable to the whims of new administrators. As new presidents and other key administrators are appointed, the commitment to critical thinking must remain. It is vitally important, therefore, to include the entire campus community in change from the start.

**Provide Ongoing Faculty and Staff Workshops.** Once administrative and key faculty support is in place, the next important step is to introduce critical thinking to the faculty at large. At the Center for Critical Thinking, we have found that the only effective way for doing this is by offering critical thinking workshops conducted by experts. These workshops should be systematically conducted with a clear design in mind and should continue throughout a five-to-seven-year period, if not longer.

Although there is no one correct way to design faculty workshops in critical thinking, some essential guidelines should be followed. Typically, the best workshop design is one that begins with an introduction to the foundations of critical thinking, which is systematically followed up by contextualization of these foundations throughout curricular areas, as well as collegewide policies and practices.

Before any workshops are conducted, or as soon as the first one has been offered, a leadership team should be identified. The primary purpose of the leadership team is to continuously deepen its understanding of critical thinking so as to eventually provide introductory workshops in critical thinking to faculty on campus. This team should include only those faculty and staff who have demonstrated commitment to long-term development as teachers, learners, and thinkers. This team, if well chosen, serves as an internal mechanism for keeping the process going as top-level administrators come and go. An effective design for faculty workshops conducted by experts in critical thinking would include at least ten days of workshops per year in a particular pattern:

• *First year, fall semester:* two days of critical thinking training that all faculty are required to attend. Three additional days of training for the leadership team (five days in all for members of the team). These sessions focus on the foundations of critical thinking, specifically the elements of reasoning, intellectual standards, intellectual virtues, and barriers to the development of thinking.

• *First year, spring semester:* two days of critical thinking training for all faculty who wish to attend. Three additional days of training for the leadership team. These sessions should focus on applying the foundations of critical thinking within subjects and disciplines, and across the curriculum.

• *Second, third, fourth, and fifth years:* the same structure should be followed as in the first year, except that faculty should be encouraged, rather than required, to attend. Workshop topics might include Socratic questioning, understanding content as a mode of thinking, learning to assess thinking within any discipline, fostering the traits of the disciplined mind, ethical reasoning, scientific reasoning, reasoning within the social sciences, historical reasoning, mathematical reasoning, professional reasoning (in a variety of fields), close reading, substantive writing, and teaching students to assess their own reasoning.

You might ask whether it is possible for a staff development program to proceed without the guidance of experts in critical thinking. The answer is theoretically yes, but practically speaking it is unlikely. The fact is that mistakes are part of learning. Feedback from experts is important for facilitating effective and accurate self-assessment. As well, experts can correct for predictable misunderstandings and misapplications.

**Create Activities and Opportunities That Foster Critical Thinking Throughout the Year.** In addition to offering workshops led by critical thinking experts, it is vital to give faculty opportunities to continue developing as thinkers and sharing classroom strategies. The plan for these activities should take into account insights introduced by the college's new experts in critical thinking. These activities might include:

A monthly newsletter inviting all faculty and staff to share thoughts and insights about critical thinking (including ways to teach for it)

A Web forum wherein faculty and staff can routinely engage in critical
thinking discussions
Planned roundtable discussions that all faculty and staff can attend, with
ever-evolving critical thinking topics
Predesigned foundational seminars for new faculty that are facilitated by the
leadership team but designed by experts in critical thinking (after the first
year)
Faculty access to publications and other resources in critical thinking

**Link Critical Thinking to Assessment, Accreditation, and the College Mission.** It is important to place critical thinking at the center of all
official college objectives, as well as its mission. Critical thinking must also
be tied to assessment of faculty, students, the college as a whole, and the
accreditation processes. This can be done in multiple ways, but the important thing is that it be done. As accrediting agencies begin to understand
what it takes to foster the concept of a Learning College, tying critical thinking to the quality of instruction becomes more obvious and more imperative.

One effective way of measuring faculty knowledge of critical thinking, as
well as the extent to which faculty are effectively teaching it, is to use an interview protocol developed by the Center for Critical Thinking (Paul, Elder, and
Bartell, 1997). This protocol can be used both in pre- and postassessments of
faculty knowledge about critical thinking. In addition, *The International Critical
Thinking Test* (Paul and Elder, 2003) can be used to assess students' reasoning
abilities. Another student assessment tool, now commonly used in community
colleges, is the Community College Survey of Student Engagement (CCSSE).
To assess the extent to which critical thinking is being fostered in the college
as a whole, random samples of student work can be obtained from across the
curriculum and then assessed for critical thinking.

**Fund the Program.** An effective staff development program cannot occur
without adequate funding, and it may be necessary to identify grant possibilities. Early in the process, a budget must be established to fund the program,
including costs for the critical thinking workshops, critical thinking materials
(books, videos, and so forth), and release time for the leadership team.

**Keep the Focus on a Substantive Concept of Critical Thinking.** One
of the pitfalls in creating a professional development program focused on thinking is the tendency to pick and choose from multiple theories of thinking, some
of which may lack rigor or breadth. Stick to a robust concept of critical thinking. No matter what else is true about teaching and learning, it is vitally important that students learn the cognitive skills to think their way through content.
This can be done only if they are encouraged to use their thinking in a disciplined way throughout their college experience. Every part of the professional
development program must work toward achieving this end.

**Avoid Political Problems.** Every college has a political dimension.
Prudently work within it without betraying the critical thinking principles
to which you are committed.

**Beware of Intellectual Arrogance.** In a large study of thirty-eight public and twenty-eight private colleges and universities (Paul, Elder, and Bartell, 1997), the Center for Critical Thinking found a significant gap between what faculty think they know about critical thinking and what classroom practices actually reveal (about what they know). Much of the gap is traceable to inadvertent intellectual arrogance. As a college begins to introduce critical thinking to faculty, it must anticipate and respond to problems that may result when faculty misteach what they have mislearned about critical thinking, either to students or to colleagues. For this reason, the advice and assistance of a critical thinking expert throughout the process is necessary.

**Avoid Elitism; Be Inclusive from the Start.** Another potential danger in creating an effective professional development program is the appearance that those heading up the program are an elite group. When this occurs, the rest of the faculty begin to define themselves in opposition. Therefore the professional development program should be, from the start, as inclusive as possible. It must encourage and challenge, but not threaten or invalidate. The next section describes how one community college has developed a professional development plan that includes many of the components discussed in this chapter.

## Surry Community College: A Professional Development Plan in Progress

For the past two years, Surry Community College (North Carolina) has been creating a professional development program based on the principles and steps outlined here. This section details this relatively new and evolving program.

**The Initial Impetus for Change.** In the fall of 2002, Surry began to think about how to place learning at the center of instruction. It did not initially identify critical thinking as the key to this process. However, Surry had been introduced to the notion of the Learning College, an idea developed by Terry O'Banion, president emeritus of the League for Innovation in the Community College, which was beginning to influence two-year colleges across the country. According to O'Banion (1999):

> It is not enough to make students feel good about the environment on the campus or the services they receive. It is not enough to impress students with the dazzling performance of great lecturers. It is not enough to provide all the latest in information technology. If we cannot document expanded or improved learning—however defined and however measured—we cannot say with any assurance that learning has occurred. And it is much more likely that we will be able to document learning when we place high value on learning-centered policies, programs, and practices and when we employ personnel who know how to create learning outcomes, learning options, and learning-centered activities [n.p.].

After reviewing the literature, Surry identified and chose to concentrate on specific facets of the Learning College:

The recognized mission of the college is student learning.
The institution accepts responsibility for student learning.
Supporting and promoting student learning is everyone's job.
Planning and operational decisions are made with consideration for their potential impact on student learning.
Transforming a college into a learning institution requires a systematic and systemic review of the organization and its people, structure, policies, and processes.

As Surry pursued the idea of the Learning College, faculty and administrators began to see critical thinking as essential to such a college.

Surry's impetus to move toward the learning college model resulted from two unrelated events. First, in December 2002 the Southern Association of Colleges and Schools adopted a major revision of its accreditation process, adding a quality enhancement component. At that same time, Surry agreed to participate as one of forty-eight colleges in the first open administration of the Community College Survey of Student Engagement (CCSSE). This survey questioned students about, among other things, the quality of their college learning experience.

Before Surry received results from this survey, faculty were asked by the administration to state how, in their view, students would respond "if Surry Community College were exactly as you would like it to be" (Atkins and Wolfe, 2003b, n.p.). According to Atkins and Wolfe, when Surry's results from the CCSSE were compared with faculty objectives for students:

> The comparison depicted a discrepancy between student reports and faculty perceptions regarding our students' engagement in critical thinking skills. Overall results indicated that faculty believe students should be engaged in critical thinking skills to a much greater extent than levels reported by students. During special CCSSE focus-group sessions, faculty identified areas they considered critical for enhancing student learning and recommended strategies for improvement. Faculty wanted students to be more active in the classroom, to more often integrate ideas and information. Critical thinking activities were consistently mentioned, as well as cross-discipline projects, capstone course projects, and writing across the curriculum. These issues would soon be transformed into major project objectives for improving student learning at Surry [2003b, n.p.].

**Creating a Culture for Change and Organizing the Change Process.**
In organizing their change process, Surry developed the Surry Community College Learning Initiative, an evolving, multifaceted approach to fostering a learning community across the campus. It aims to establish structures, policies, leadership practices, professional development, and curriculum

initiatives that improve student learning (Atkins and Wolfe, 2003a). The Surry Learning Initiative commits the college to thoroughly assessing its organizational culture to determine features that support or hinder the move to a more learning-centered college; ensuring that college leaders, both academic and administrative, substantively support learning-centered initiatives; enacting academic policies to reflect an emphasis on learning; creating decision-making structures to ensure involvement of all key stakeholders; and revising the language in all appropriate documents (mission statements, program descriptions, job descriptions) to reflect the new emphasis on learning (Atkins and Wolfe, 2003a).

**The College Establishes a Guiding Council and Primary Objectives.** After creating a culture for change and organizing the change process, Surry established a Council on Innovation and Student Learning, a steering committee responsible for guiding the change process. This council comprises all division chairs, the vice president for instruction and chief academic officer, the president of the college, and representatives from all student support departments. The council involves the entire college community in deciding upon specific strategies for improving learning (Atkins and Wolfe, 2003a). Early in the change process, the council established three objectives: improve student engagement through critical thinking, assess learning outcomes, and reform organizational culture.

**Critical Thinking Becomes the Key to the Learning College.** Early on, critical thinking was listed as one of several primary objectives by Surry faculty. However, it was not initially considered central to the change process. According to the director of the academic support center, "We discussed the fact that we couldn't focus on all eight outcomes at once, that we'd have to introduce them slowly. We decided that critical thinking would be a good place to start—since it was at the top of the faculty list. . . . One of our first goals, then, was to investigate critical thinking models and professional development opportunities" (Connie Wolfe, personal correspondence, Sept. 2004).

As Surry began to formulate a rigorous concept of critical thinking, it became clear that the only way to create a substantive Learning College, with true emphasis on developing intellectual skills, was through critical thinking. Conversely, it also became clear that without critical thinking the Learning College would be devoid of substance and depth. According to Wolfe, as Surry began to understand critical thinking:

> Many things fell into place. We began to see how critical thinking was important for all the QEP objectives—improving student engagement, improving student learning and evaluating that learning, and reforming college culture. . . . We are now using critical thinking as the substantive concept that guides instruction and improves learning. . . . After receiving critical thinking training, I felt that the learning college model didn't give us the whole picture. In fact, I've been surprised that other colleges haven't connected critical

thinking to the learning college more often. Everyone talks about improving critical thinking, and many colleges see value in the learning paradigm, but putting the two together into a coherent plan for improvement hasn't been a major focus (that I know of). I look at the list [of the Learning College Project] and wonder if we could do all those things and *still* not fundamentally improve the quality of student learning! The fundamental question is this: How are we actually changing what we're doing in the classroom to improve student learning? Critical thinking has become our vehicle for doing just that. The deeper we get into this plan, the more we find ourselves focusing on critical thinking. We have just now realized the extent to which we're going to have to do professional development, the extent to which we're still critical thinking neophytes (even after advanced training!). We recognize we must constantly assess what we're doing and make changes as a result, and that the entire college community (all employees and students) must participate and own it for themselves, or we won't see real change [Wolfe, personal correspondence, Aug. 2004].

**Coordinating and Providing Faculty Workshops in Critical Thinking.** An ongoing part of Surry's professional development plan is faculty workshops in critical thinking. A long-term in-service program in critical thinking has been developed, with workshops on several of the topics listed earlier in this chapter. In addition to these workshops, Surry's Team for the Advancement of Critical Thinking is conducting introductory workshops for faculty throughout the year. Experts in critical thinking will assist Surry in predesigning and assessing these workshops.

**A Summary of the Surry Professional Development Program.** The first key component of Surry's approach is that the program began with the commitment of senior administrators. The vice president for instruction and chief academic officer not only spearheaded the project but took time to learn critical thinking and has, at present, participated as a learner in fourteen days of critical thinking training. Moreover, he is taking a lead role in facilitating the predesigned workshops for faculty and staff. As well, senior administrators at Surry have committed significant resources and time to the process. Further, an advisory council was formed to guide and integrate the process. Early in the process, faculty were asked to identify important learning outcomes for students.

In addition, faculty and staff work together on various committees to infuse critical thinking into the entire campus culture, and experts in critical thinking are holding workshops in critical thinking over several years. A leadership team is learning critical thinking so they can serve as facilitators in workshops for faculty and staff throughout the year. Critical thinking is tied to assessment through an institutional portfolio that randomly selects student papers from across the campus and assesses them using critical thinking concepts and principles. Faculty assessments are also tied to critical thinking, and faculty are required to submit sample assignments demonstrating that they are fostering critical thinking in their classes. These assignments are then evaluated, and faculty are given feedback and suggestions for improvement where necessary. As well, roundtable discussions that focus on critical thinking theory and classroom application are offered throughout the year. Both a newsletter and a Website have been developed as forums for progress reports, updates, and discussions.

## Conclusion

It is possible, certainly, to create a *true* learning college, one that cultivates the intellect, and that fosters acquisition of substantive and lasting knowledge. But this can be done only with a well-designed plan that evolves as it is carried out; a plan that presupposes a substantive concept of critical thinking, that has a sufficient dose of intellectual humility, and that includes true and lasting administrative commitment and support.

## References

Atkins, S., and Wolfe, C. "The Surry Community College Learning Initiative: Creating a Learning-Centered College by Improving Student Engagement Through Critical Thinking, Assessing Learning Outcomes, and Reforming Organizational Culture." Dobson, N.C.: Surry Community College, 2003a.

Atkins, S., and Wolfe, C. "Toward a New Way of Thinking and Learning: Becoming a Learning College." *Learning Abstracts,* 2003b, 6(9), n.p. http://www.league.org/publication/abstracts/learning/lelabs0309.htm. Accessed Feb. 10, 2005.

O'Banion, T. "The Learning College: Both Learner and Learning Centered." *Learning Abstracts, World Wide Web Edition,* 1999, 2(2), n.p. http://www.league.org/publication/abstracts/learning/lelabs9903.html. Accessed Feb. 14, 2005.

Paul, R. "Teaching That Cultivates the Intellect." Conference brochure, 25th International Conference on Critical Thinking and Education Reform. Dillon Beach, Calif.: Foundation for Critical Thinking, Spring 2004.

Paul, R., and Elder, L. *The International Critical Thinking Test.* Dillon Beach, Calif.: Foundation for Critical Thinking, 2003.

Paul, R., Elder, L., and Bartell, T. *California Teacher Preparation for Instruction in Critical Thinking: Research Finding and Recommendations.* Sacramento: California Commission on Teacher Credentialing, 1997.

LINDA ELDER *is an educational psychologist and president of the Foundation for Critical Thinking, a nonprofit education organization in Dillon Beach, California.*

5

*Teaching critical thinking in community college classrooms involves helping students overcome emotional barriers and question and critique commonly held assumptions.*

# Overcoming Impostorship, Cultural Suicide, and Lost Innocence: Implications for Teaching Critical Thinking in the Community College

*Stephen D. Brookfield*

Critical thinking occupies a special place in the hearts of many community college teachers who regard the skills endemic to it—particularly identifying and scrutinizing assumptions—as foundational elements of lifelong learning. Critical thinking is also deemed to be important because of its connection to the democratic tradition. At the heart of a strong, participatory democracy is citizens' capacity to question the actions, justifications, and decisions of political leaders, and their capacity to imagine alternatives to current structures and moralities that are fairer and more compassionate. Such capacities are judged by some to develop as we learn to think critically. Consequently, encouraging critical thinking is often seen as integral to the democratic project. Critical thinking is also pursued because learning to think critically can help students deal with ambiguity and negotiate the bewildering pace of social and technological change.

Critical thinking involves recognizing and researching the assumptions that undergird our thoughts and actions. Assumptions are our taken-for-granted beliefs about the world and our place within it; they seem so obvious to us as not to need to be stated explicitly. Assumptions give meaning and purpose to who we are and what we do. In many ways, we *are* our assumptions. So much of what we think, say, and do is based on assumptions about how the world should work and what counts as appropriate, moral action within it. Yet frequently these assumptions are not recognized for the provisional understandings that they really are. Ideas and actions that we regard as commonsense conventional wisdom are often based on uncritically accepted assumptions. Some person, institution, or authority that we either trust or fear has told us that "this is the way things are" and we accept their judgment unquestioningly. Critical thinking, at its core, is the process of hunting down and checking these assumptions.

When we think critically, we research our assumptions for the evidence and experiences that inform them. Sometimes we find these assumptions are justified by our (or others') experience, in which case we feel a confidence in their accuracy and validity. If we can say why we hold an assumption, and if we can cite the experiences it's grounded in, we possess an informed commitment to it. At other times, however, we find that our assumptions are flawed, distorted, or accurate only within a much narrower range of situations than we had originally thought. When this happens, we realize we need to abandon or reframe these assumptions so that they constitute a more accurate guide to, and justification for, our actions.

The process of critical thinking usually begins with an event that points out a discrepancy between assumptions and perspectives that we believe explain the world satisfactorily, and an awareness that this is not in fact the case. Students identify the assumptions that they have accepted unquestioningly up to that event, and start to scrutinize them for their accuracy and validity. During this process of scrutiny, alternative perspectives suggest themselves. The final phase of the cycle is taking informed action. Informed action is grounded in an accurate assessment of the context in which the action will occur, so that the anticipated consequences of the action are as close as possible to those that actually occur. It is also action for which an informed rationale, and appropriate evidence, can be given. Action, as understood here, is cognitive as well as behavioral. For example, the result of critical thinking about the prospects for successful social change might be the decision to refrain from becoming involved in a change initiative until sufficient resources have been assembled and strong alliances built.

Thinking critically often involves taking a perspective on social and political structures, or on personal and collective actions, that is strongly alternative to majority, commonsense wisdom. The political underpinning to much work on critical thinking urges students to analyze commonly held ideas for the extent to which they perpetuate economic inequity, deny compassion, foster a culture of silence, and prevent people from realizing their common interests. This is often risky since it brings people face-to-face with the power structures that create and perpetuate dominant cultural values and worldviews.

## Students' Experiences of Learning to Think Critically

Teaching critical thinking in the community college is most effectively grounded in analysis of how students experience this learning process. Learning to think critically is difficult for many students as they contemplate the move from dichotomous, universalistic forms of thinking to multifaceted, contextual forms. In previous research I have published on this topic (Brookfield, 1987, 1994, 1995), together with hundreds of firsthand testimonies I have collected from students over the years, certain predictable emotional rhythms of learning critical thinking can be discerned. Chief among these are impostorship, cultural suicide, and lost innocence.

**Impostorship.** Impostorship occurs when students feel, at some deeply embedded level, that they possess neither the talent nor the right to become critical thinkers. When asked to undertake a critical analysis of ideas propounded by people seen as experts, learners often feel that to do so smacks of temerity and impertinence (Brookfield, 1993). More particularly, they report that their own experience is so limited that it gives them no starting point from which to build an academic critique of authorities in their field of study. There is a kind of steamrolling effect in which the status of "theorist" or "major figure" flattens students' fledgling critical antennae. This is perhaps most evident when the figures concerned are heroic in their eyes, but it is also obvious when students are faced with a piece of work in which the bibliographic scholarship is seen as impressive or a skill demonstration is at an extremely high level of proficiency. The sense of impostorship students feel in daring to comment critically on such work or practice makes their attempt at critical analysis seem a rather unconvincing form of play acting. Their assumption is that any critique they produce will be revealed to be the product of an unfit mind.

**Cultural Suicide.** Cultural suicide is what often happens to learners who are in the critical process and who are seen by those around them to be reinventing themselves. In cultural suicide, students perceive that if they take a critical questioning of conventional assumptions, justifications, structures, and actions too far they will risk being excluded from the culture that has defined and sustained them up to that point in their life. The perception of this danger, and experience of its actuality, is a common theme in community college students' autobiographies. The student in a critical process who was formerly seen by friends and intimates as "one of us" may be seen as having betrayed, or left behind, his or her peers. The critical thinker is viewed as taking on airs and pretension, as growing "too big for her boots," or as aspiring to the status of intellectual in contrast to her friends and colleagues who feel they are now perceived as less sophisticated creatures. The learner who has come to a critical awareness of what most people take for granted can pose a real threat to those who are not on a similar journey of self-discovery, or who do not see themselves as engaged in the same political or intellectual project. In the eyes of those left behind, the critically aware student is perceived as having "gone native," or having become a full-fledged member of the tribal culture of academe.

**Loss of Innocence.** Students in critical process speak of the epistemological as well as the cultural risks they run, and they see their learning to think critically as a journey into ambiguity and uncertainty. Such travel requires a willingness to let go of eternal verities and the reassuring prospect of eventual truth. In particular, students speak of a loss of innocence, innocence in this case being a belief in the promise that if they study hard and look long enough they will stumble on universal truth as the reward for all their efforts. People in critical process look back to their time as dualistic thinkers—and to their faith that if they just put enough effort into solving problems, solutions would always appear—as a golden era of certainty. An intellectual appreciation of the importance of contextuality and ambiguity comes to exist alongside a visceral craving for certainty.

**Peer Support.** As learners speak of their own critical process, they also attest to the importance of their belonging to an emotionally sustaining peer learning community—a group of colleagues who are also experiencing dissonance, reinterpreting their practice, challenging old assumptions, and falling afoul of conservative forces. Given the fluctuating, emotionally complex, and culturally punishing nature of critical thinking, it is not surprising to hear learners speak of the store they place on this membership in a peer support group. In talking and writing about the factors that help them sustain momentum through the lowest moments in their autobiography as a critical learner, it is this membership in a learning community—an emotionally sustaining group of peers—that is mentioned more consistently than anything else. These groups are spoken of as "a second family," "the only people who really understand what I'm going through," "my partners in crime"; they constitute a safe haven in which critical learners can confirm they are not alone, and through which they can make sense of the changes they are experiencing.

## Experientially Grounded Approaches to Teaching Critical Thinking

What do students' experiences of learning to think critically mean for our practice as educators? Student accounts suggest five broad implications for teaching critical thinking in the community college.

**Build a Case for Critical Thinking.** The first implication is the need to build a case for critical thinking. A major mistake faculty often make is to assume that students share their conviction regarding the importance of critical thinking. This unchecked assumption needs serious critical examination. Community college students who are using education as a means to change a career are likely to be impatient with any instruction that does not appear to lead directly to employment or enhanced career opportunity. Couple this with the behavior learned in high school that the teacher is an authoritative source of knowledge who bestows unambiguous answers, and you realize the perception that critical thinking is important is far from universal.

Several strategies are helpful in building a case for the importance of critical thinking. Faculty can bring former students into the classroom to talk about the important role critical thinking has played in their studies or work responsibilities. When I begin a new course where I know critical thinking will be resisted, I try to invite former students into the first class to form a visiting panel of experts. These former students each talk briefly about the importance that learning to think critically has had in their own life. In doing this, they are likely to use examples from their own autobiography that are framed in language that new students find more convincing than anything I could say. It is enormously powerful for newly enrolled, resistant students to hear formerly resistant students say that they never would have made it through college without being able to think critically, or that without the capacity to scrutinize assumptions they would have done something at work that would have gotten them fired.

Simulations and case studies can also be employed early on to build an experiential case for critical thinking. The scenario analysis and crisis decision simulations I describe later in this chapter are two examples of exercises I commonly use. Of course, a key component of such simulations and case studies is that students can only resolve them successfully by researching an assumption they have previously taken for granted, or viewing familiar ideas or practices from a new perspective (the core elements of critical thinking).

**Model Critical Thinking.** It is also important to model critical thinking to students. Students consistently report that a crucial element in their learning to think critically is seeing faculty demonstrate their engagement in the process. Such modeling is done in a number of ways. In team-taught courses, faculty can demonstrate respectful critique of each other's position and practice. In solo-taught courses, faculty can use the critical incident questionnaire as a classroom research tool to demonstrate how they are using students' perspectives to undertake a critical analysis of their own assumptions regarding classroom practice.

The critical incident questionnaire is a five-item sheet that students fill out anonymously once a week. The questionnaire asks about engaging and distancing classroom moments, as well as helpful or puzzling classroom actions. The five questions are, At what moment this week were you most engaged as a learner? At what moment this week were you most distanced as a learner? What action that anyone (teacher or student) took this week was most affirming or helpful to you as a learner? What action that anyone (teacher or student) took this week was most confusing or puzzling to you as a learner? What surprised you most about the class this week? (See Brookfield, 1995, for further discussion and application of this instrument.)

Faculty collect the questionnaires, read and analyze them, and then begin the next week's classes by giving a summary of the chief responses on the sheets. During this summary, teachers can talk about the assumptions that were confirmed or challenged by learner responses and point out that they are engaging in critical thinking about their own practice (Brookfield, 1995).

Faculty who rely on the lecture method can also model critical thinking by making sure they end their lecture with a summary of the questions that could be raised concerning their lecture assertions. Ending with a summary of what has already been said (the usual pattern lecturers follow) establishes too much of a sense of definitive closure. A helpful practice is for lecturers to end their presentation by pointing out all the new questions that have been raised for them by the content of the lecture, and by pointing out which of the questions posed at the start of the lecture have been left unanswered or have been reframed more provocatively or contentiously.

During the lecture itself, faculty can play devil's advocate by regularly moving to another part of the lecture room, turning back toward where they were previously standing, and then pointing out everything that was flawed, ambiguous, uncertain, or ethically questionable about what they have just said. They can also note the chief ideas or information they omitted because it was inconvenient to the central tenets of the lecture. As they do this, faculty can remind students that they are engaging in critical thinking, and they can also tell students that later in the course faculty are going to ask students to engage in this same process.

**Place Students in Peer Groups.** A third pedagogic practice is placing students in peer learning communities. As students work their way through critical thinking episodes, they frequently mention how often they use other people—teachers, peers, friends, family members, work colleagues, experts—as their chief learning resources. Students speak of critical thinking as a social learning process in which others serve as a critically reflective mirror. Any critical thinking initiative can build on this idea by situating critical thinking in a peer learning circle. In critical thinking exercises such as critical conversation protocol, circular response, circle of voices, and critical debate, the discussion group is the crucible for critical thinking (Brookfield and Preskill, 1999). All these exercises require participation, and all structure it to ensure every student gets a chance to speak.

Developing community can occur in a number of ways. Asking students to introduce each other, rather than introduce themselves, is a useful icebreaker at the beginning of a course. At the start of a class, faculty can also compile and distribute a course register of student names and addresses that includes description of students' personal interests and work responsibilities. At the urban, commuter campus where I worked in New York, I used to ask students to put on the blackboard the subway routes they used to journey to and from campus. Because the campus was located in a neighborhood then viewed by out-of-towners as somewhat unsafe, I suggested that students form walking and subway groups according to traveling routes they had in common. My hope (subsequently confirmed) was that while walking to and from the subway or riding on it students would talk about the one thing they had in common: their identity as a student in my class.

Cohort-based programs have a built-in tendency to create community, but noncohort classes also have opportunities for community building. Pedagogically, any use of team projects or team presentations is often a useful spur to developing community. I currently teach a class where students put on a miniconference during the last few sessions of the course. The teams who present at these sessions are formed early in the course on the basis of student expressions of interest. I give time for planning team presentations in class, in the hope that such activity will build more personal relationships among learners. Whenever I use small-group discussion methods in class, I am also careful to employ exercises that democratize participation and allow all members to be heard. Typical ground rules are that members must make conversational moves that show appreciation for the contribution of others, or that any comments made must refer only to something that has already been said by another member.

**Ground Critical Thinking in Specific Experiences.** One of the problems in teaching critical thinking is that students are unused to the abstract modes of thought required to uncover assumptions. This brings us to our fourth implication, the need to ground critical thinking in analysis of specific experience. Instead of asking learners to respond to the question, "What assumptions do you hold?" it is far more productive to ask them to focus on concrete events. Teachers of critical thinking are advised to use a critical incident approach, in which students uncover and research their assumptions by exploring a particular moment, situation, or incident in their life.

For example, asking students to talk about assumptions underlying what it means to be a good parent, a good friend, or a good worker more often than not produces a series of socially sanctioned clichés. But ask students to choose the day in the last month on which they felt proudest of their parenting, or when they felt they accomplished a feat that deserved the "Employee of the Month" award, and you have something much meatier to explore. As students talk about specific details such as where and when the event happened, who was involved, and what was most memorable about the occurrence, teachers have much more productive material for analysis. The sequence of teaching events described later in this chapter illustrates this emphasis on concrete events.

**Think of Critical Thinking as Incremental Movements.** Finally, thinking critically about our ideas or practices is, in intellectual terms, akin to running an Olympic-level 100-yard sprint. Just as a nonrunner would not contemplate participating in such an event without a substantial amount of training, so uncritical thinkers cannot contemplate direct, critical analysis of their own ideas or experiences without being adequately prepared for it. Nonathletes will tear a hamstring if they participate in a 100-yard sprint without extensive warming up. Similarly, noncritical thinkers will seriously damage their intellectual muscles if they do not ease into the process. We need to consider critical thinking as an incremental movement in which learners begin far away from their own ideas and experiences and gradually move to direct analysis of them. This means that students must first learn the mental protocol of identifying and researching assumptions (often by looking at familiar ideas and actions from a distinctly unfamiliar vantage point) in settings that are nonpersonal and therefore nonthreatening. As the process of assumption hunting becomes ingrained, they can gradually apply a critical thinking protocol to their own ideas and experiences. But to start students at this point risks a massive tearing of intellectual hamstrings.

One particular sequence of exercises I have used in my own practice illustrates the incremental process of teaching critical thinking. Learners begin the sequence by engaging in scenario analysis, imagining themselves in the position of the chief actor in a fictional scenario. They try to uncover the implicit and explicit assumptions under which the actor is operating, assess how these assumptions might be checked, and come up with plausible alternative interpretations of the scenario. Crisis decision simulation is the second stage in the sequence. In small groups, learners discuss how to resolve a fictional crisis in a short time (for example, which person in an overloaded lifeboat should be abandoned to save the rest). In debriefing their response to this simulation, each group analyzes the assumptions underlying its decision and attempts to uncover and scrutinize its inferential ladder.

The third exercise in the sequence is titled "Heroes/Heroines and Villains/Villainesses." Here learners choose a colleague they particularly admire (or despise) and identify an example of that person's behavior that encapsulates what is so admirable (or despicable) about them. The choice appears to be focused on other people but is actually very revealing about many of their own assumptions. Fourth, students continue the sequence by engaging in a focused critical conversation in which one person's experience (that of the storyteller) is examined sympathetically but critically by colleagues (the detectives). An umpire watches for judgmental comment (Brookfield and Preskill, 1999).

The final phase in this incremental sequence of critical thinking is the Good Practices Audit (Brookfield, 1995). This exercise takes several days during which students identify problems that impede them and then work collaboratively to examine their own and their colleagues' experiences as practitioners and learners in a structured and critical way. The intent is to use this analysis as a prompt to proposing responses and possible resolutions to the problems initially identified.

## Conclusion

Several criticisms can be leveled at the literature on critical thinking. One concerns the Eurocentric bias of the research and theoretical base. The most-cited authorities are all white, European, and male, and the samples informing their theorizing are overwhelmingly white Anglo-Americans. Additionally, critical thinking elevates a Western form of cognitive, rational knowing above other forms of comprehension. There is little attention paid to affect, emotion, spirituality, or holistic modes of being and knowing.

Similarly, little consideration is given to how critical reflection can be triggered through aesthetic experiences, meditation, and contemplation.

Critical thinking is sometimes conceived in a masculinist way as an exclusionary, inherently skeptical form of separate knowing. Furthermore, the recent upsurge of postmodernist thought has questioned the linear, developmental manner in which narratives of critical thinking ("I was uncritical, took a course, and became critical") are often presented. Such a narrative is deemed by postmodernists to be purely a fictional construct in which the learner is cast as a hero struggling successfully to purge demons of racism and sexism. Finally, critical thinking literature has been criticized for overly exclusionary language that intimidates many of the learners it seeks to help.

Despite these criticisms, the idea of critical thinking continues to hold a powerful sway on the imagination of the community college educator. Those who seek to develop it in students would be well advised to build on what students themselves say about how they move through its rhythms. Methodologically, this can be called a position of critical pragmatism. Instead of working from a previously articulated theoretical model, a truly critical approach to developing critical thought grounds itself in the experiences of students and seeks constantly to adjust to them.

## References

Brookfield, S. D. *Developing Critical Thinkers: Challenging Adults to Explore Alternative Ways of Thinking and Acting.* San Francisco: Jossey-Bass, 1987.

Brookfield, S. D. "Breaking the Code: Engaging Practitioners in Critical Analysis of Adult Educational Literature." *Studies in the Education of Adults,* 1993, 25(1), 64–91.

Brookfield, S. D. "Tales from the Dark Side: A Phenomenography of Adult Critical Reflection." *International Journal of Lifelong Education,* 1994, 13(3), 203–216.

Brookfield, S. D. *Becoming a Critically Reflective Teacher.* San Francisco: Jossey-Bass, 1995.

Brookfield, S. D., and Preskill, S. *Discussion as a Way of Teaching: Tools and Techniques for Democratic Classrooms.* San Francisco: Jossey-Bass, 1999.

STEPHEN D. BROOKFIELD *is a distinguished professor at the University of St. Thomas in Minneapolis-St. Paul.*

6

*Two common models of teaching critical thinking in a discipline fail to do justice to the essential role critical thinking plays in all learning or to its role in the discipline as a whole. This chapter describes a model that emphasizes a more central role for critical thinking in shaping all course activity and in focusing on the most fundamental and powerful discipline-based concepts.*

# Problems with Two Standard Models for Teaching Critical Thinking

*Gerald M. Nosich*

This chapter focuses on two major questions about teaching for critical thinking. First, how deeply should critical thinking extend into the community college classroom? For example, what portion of a class should be devoted to teaching students to think critically as opposed to, say, giving them content information, or targeting other goals such as student engagement? The second question is related: If the goal of the course is to teach students to think critically in a discipline, which topics within the discipline should be targeted and covered?

These questions are directly related to two standard models for incorporating critical thinking into community college courses. Both of them, in the end, do a disservice to critical thinking, and consequently to students' ability to think within a field or subject matter. This chapter discusses these two common methods of teaching for critical thinking in a discipline and then presents a model that emphasizes a more central role for critical thinking in shaping all course activity and in focusing on the most fundamental and powerful concepts in the discipline. Although the remarks in this chapter are directed at critical thinking instruction in community colleges, a recent study by Paul, Elder, and Bartell (1997) demonstrates that the critiques apply equally to four-year institutions.

---

I wish to thank Richard Paul and Linda Elder for extensive discussion, analysis, and evaluation of all aspects of critical thinking over the years, including the ideas in this chapter.

## "One of Many" Model

Perhaps the most common method of teaching for critical thinking in a discipline can be called the "one-of-many" model. In it, an instructor teaches by making critical thinking a part of the class but also uses a number of other ways to help students learn material. In this model, critical thinking is only one method among many for helping students learn the subject matter. A teacher following this method might describe their course in this way:

> I require my students to engage in critical thinking in my classes. In fact, I devote fifteen minutes per class period to having my students think critically in various ways: small-group discussion, critical writing, answering *why* questions, supporting answers with reasons, and identifying conflicting points of view. But in addition, I also have students engage in other ways of learning the material. I have them memorize information when it is appropriate. I have them learn to follow step-by-step procedures without having to think critically about them. I construct activities to help them become more engaged with the material, and in those activities I am not concerned with whether they are employing higher-order thinking skills.

Virtually any textbook in any field bears witness to this model of teaching. Exercises at the end of a chapter typically include three distinct sections. First, there are questions that require pure recall of terms or rote application of a procedure; they are to be answered by direct reference to the text (usually only to boldfaced terms, and usually only to terms or calculations from that particular chapter). Students completing these exercises are not required to process the meaning of a term or procedure, or the relation or link with concepts from other chapters, let alone concepts from other courses. Second, there are questions that are called or can loosely be described as critical thinking questions. Third, there are engagement questions, in some texts at least, that are designed to help students connect the chapter topic to their life. These questions lack, however, any directions about how to carry out this engagement *critically*.

Analysis of twenty-four major texts frequently used in community college instruction dramatically illustrates massive emphasis on rote learning. The analyzed texts are in seventeen disciplines, including those within composition, literature and the arts, social sciences, education, natural sciences, business, information systems, and math. All twenty-four texts include exercises listing key terms to be memorized (sometimes as many as eighty-eight "key" terms in a single chapter!), questions to answer by pure recall, or problems to solve by using rote application of a procedure (although sometimes, especially in math or the sciences, the procedure is complicated). Of the texts sampled, only seventeen contained any critical thinking questions, and only twelve contained engagement questions.

Interestingly, recall items in the texts are identified by various names—although they seem never to be labeled "recall questions" or "rote application." They are often called "key terms" or "review questions." One major biology text called this section "understanding the basics," despite the fact that no understanding is required, only recall. A widely adopted psychology text even has a section called "critical thinking exercise," yet the questions simply required rote application of a procedure.

The average number of recall items per textbook exercise at the end of a chapter was 46; the average number of critical thinking–related items was 5; the average number of engagement items was 2.5. Textbook exercises thus show critical thinking to be only one, relatively minor, aspect of learning a discipline.

## "Cover As Much Content As Possible" Model

In the second model of teaching, content is conceptualized as a long list of concepts and ideas, ranging from the most central or overarching down to the most specific and peripheral. From this range of ideas on every level, teachers select questions and problems for students to focus on, usually in the order in which they were presented in the textbook. Teachers may or may not use individual critical thinking activities to promote understanding of selected instances of these concepts and ideas.

A teacher might describe a "cover as much content as possible" course in this way:

> This is an introductory-level course in sociology. Following a best-selling textbook in the field, students study such topics as the sociological perspective (Chapter 1), sociological investigation (Chapter 2), culture (Chapter 3), society, socialization, deviance, sexuality, and so forth—twenty-three chapters in all. This week we will be studying Chapter 18, on the family. In it, students are responsible for learning nine major subtopics, including marriage patterns, theoretical analyses of the family, stages of family life, and U.S. families. This last topic contains important subsections on class, race, and gender. I have students engage in critical thinking discussion groups often. This week they will be discussing many aspects of the family, including social benefits of endogamy versus exogamy, different patterns of descent and locality (patrilineal, matrilineal, and bilateral descent; patrilocality, matrilocality, and neolocality), varieties of polygamy and monogamy, and so forth.

This second model of teaching can also be illustrated using the same sampling of major textbooks. The twenty-three texts in which it was possible to get an approximate count contain an average of 650 "key" terms, the range being from a low of 120 (in a history text) to a high of 3,600 (in a biology text). Key terms vary from ones as fundamental and central as *plate tectonics* and *continental drift* to others as specific and narrow as *barchanoid dunes.* All are indiscriminately listed as "important" or "key." Textbooks thus fit well with a model of teaching where the goal is to cover as much content as possible, with no clear delineation between what is central and what is peripheral.

## Neither Model Does Justice to Critical Thinking

Both models may incorporate critical thinking activities into instruction, but they employ a nonsubstantive concept of critical thinking (see Chapter Three in this volume). The "one of many model" makes the assumption that there are *other* viable, effective ways for students to learn the material besides learning to think their way through it. This assumption does not do justice to the centrality of critical thinking in all genuine learning. The "cover as much content as possible model" makes the assumption that students learn to think critically within the discipline and grasp how its parts relate to one another by working on a large number of discrete, circumscribed, and unsystematically chosen topics. This assumption does not do justice to the central role of fundamental concepts and ideas in learning to think within and through a discipline.

There are at least three general reasons these assumptions are misguided. Taking these reasons seriously shows that teaching for critical thinking needs to be all-pervasive; *all* content, procedures, and engagement activities must be looked at from the point of view of "How will this help my students' ability to think critically through the subject matter?" Taking the reasons seriously also shows that instruction in a discipline needs to be both functional and systematic, focused on teaching students how to use fundamental, discipline-based concepts as tools that can be used to think through virtually any topic in the subject matter.

**Noncritical Thinking Techniques Are Inadvertently Anticritical.** When asked about the desirability of teaching their students to think better, community college faculty often describe themselves as having a *choice* between teaching for critical thinking and teaching for some desirable ends other than critical thinking, such as content, information, proper procedure, or student engagement.

There is, of course, nothing wrong with these goals. It is crucially important for students to be able to grasp content, be well informed in a discipline, be able to carry out necessary procedures, be engaged in learning, and relate the subject matter to their own lives and future. These goals are not in any way misguided.

What is misguided, however, is the idea that we can teach for these goals effectively by using methods that do not require critical thinking. A critical, thoughtful method of teaching for information retention or for mastery of essential procedures includes viewing these goals through the lens of a substantive concept of critical thinking, and thus to teach them as ways of addressing important problems or questions that students must figure out. A critical method of helping students become engaged with a discipline is (again in line with a substantive concept of critical thinking) helping them learn to think through the consequences that a particular discipline has for issues that actually matter to the students. When students reason out how the subject matter conflicts with or reshapes their own real-life goals, assumptions, decisions, and points of view, they become engaged with the subject matter.

Consider memorizing information as an example. Contrary to what one might suppose, teaching students to memorize information does not lay a foundation of knowledge about which students can think critically in the next portion of the class. Such a method is not *neutral* with respect to fostering students' critical thinking abilities; it is *negative*. It fosters an uncritical idea of information itself: that information is just a set of words, arranged by someone else, divorced from the contexts in which it can be put to use. Such a method assumes that one can have information without interpreting it, without conceptualizing it themselves, without evaluating whether it is accurate (and how one might check), without assessing the problems to which it is relevant, or even whether it is clear. A parallel case can be made about learning to follow procedures by rote.

If information and procedures are not to be merely verbal and temporary, they must be learned by having students understand them—clarify them, discuss difficulties with them, interpret them—as part of a whole web of beliefs and actions. Noncritical thinking portions of a course inevitably downplay the importance of understanding information, and of following procedures thoughtfully. They downplay education that is built on understanding. To say that information or a procedure is important means that students need to be able to *grasp* it, not just memorize the right words or the right formulas—to think it through and to think through other topics using it. All thinking has to be seen as something that has a purpose; we gather information and use procedures for a purpose, as something that has implications, and as something that exists in a system of concepts. Thinking subject matter through in this way is critical thinking.

The same holds true with respect to engagement. Teachers want their students to be engaged in their learning. A best-selling sociology text asks students to "spend an hour or two with married people of different generations" because they "can be a wonderful source of information about changes in marriage and the family" (Macionis, 2001, p. 487). Notice how uncritical such engagement is. To take just one aspect, the exercise promotes the anticritical idea that testimony is automatically accurate (rather than being a valuable piece of evidence that must be evaluated); married people of differing generations can also be a potent source of *mis*information. Critical engagement involves applying both standards of reasoning and concepts in the discipline to the fabric of one's life.

**Students' Concepts Have Already Been Shaped By Noncritical Thinking.** The assumption that students can learn a subject without learning to think critically about it—that they can "learn math" merely by solving assigned problems, without learning to think mathematically—misreads the central role that thinking plays in all learning. As a result, it ignores the history of noncritical thinking that is already present in students' understanding before they even start their community college coursework.

It can often seem as if students come into a course without any beliefs about the subject matter and without any structures by which to grasp the discipline. Indeed, teachers often describe their students in exactly those terms. They often speak of their students as entering the course with no (or at least very little) knowledge of biology, or social science, or composition, or business, or speech. Described this way, one can see why teachers sometimes suppose that students are passive recipients of knowledge. If students come in as a blank slate, knowing nothing or very little of the field, it almost seems to make sense that a teacher's job is to teach them didactically, filling them with knowledge by sheer lecture and rote learning.

But of course that assumption does not hold; we have come to see that students do not learn this way. A good part of the reason the didactic approach does not work is that students are not a blank slate; they do not enter a course with "no knowledge" related to the subject. A more accurate and less misleading statement might be that students come into a class with little *accurate, connected* knowledge about the subject, or with few *appropriate structures* for understanding the discipline. They enter the course with background ideas and conceptions—unarticulated but in place—about *all* subject matter. They have an account inside them of how living things work, of why people act the way they do socially, of how business functions, of how important writing is or is not.

These background conceptions are the product of unreflective thinking: rough generalizations, wishes turned into beliefs, hand-me-down explanations, jumped-to conclusions, prejudices, folk beliefs turned into dogma, and early school experiences. They are products of a hodgepodge of thinking, both personal and cultural, and this unexamined thinking filters and interprets the discipline students are attempting to learn.

Some of the thinking embedded in background conceptions is critical; much of it is not. For example, students (and people in general) often believe there is a life force that makes living things alive; that they themselves are largely unaffected by social forces (although they believe other people certainly are influenced by them); that all points of view are equally justified; that business mostly functions through sheer desire rather than through business skills; that basic science is not really needed for nursing or other health-related fields; and that effective writing is both unimportant and impossible to learn anyway. What is more, the background accounts people bring to their course do not consist simply of information. There is *a logic* to them, which is sometimes correct, sometimes erroneous, sometimes clear, and sometimes unclear. Students bring with them a whole way of thinking about living things, the role of science, business, and writing.

Thus learning to educate students is not learning how to write on a blank slate. It is a far deeper and more entrenched problem. If I am going to teach my students Newton's laws of motion, say, and have them understand and internalize what they learn, first I have to get them to confront the non-Newtonian background account they already have in place about how things move. Then I have to help them reason out for themselves— construct their own learning—that Newton's laws are a more accurate and effective way to think about motion than the way they already have inside their head.

Critical thinking is essential for this. Unless I can help my students learn to think clearly, accurately, and relevantly about motion, they will never be able to confront the logic of their background account. They will simply learn to repeat the right words and apply little-understood algorithms to the teacher's carefully selected problems. Unless I teach my students to think critically, they will interpret all information I give them in terms of their own background logic; they will, as a result, leave the course with their basic system of beliefs alive and well.

**Students Need to Learn to Think in Terms of Central Concepts, Across the Community College Curriculum.** The "cover as much content as possible model" offers one answer to the second question in this chapter: Given a commitment to critical thinking, which topics should a teacher have students address using critical thinking? It addresses the question, however, by ignoring the systematic nature of thinking within a discipline. To teach students to think effectively in a discipline, faculty must always focus on what is most central in a course. That is, they should key in on those fundamental and powerful concepts, crucial ideas, and unifying structures by which students can begin to grasp how the discipline works as a whole, how its parts fit together.

One big problem students have in a class is grasping the discipline as a whole, understanding what is central and what is peripheral; they have trouble seeing how the parts fit together and seeing the parts in terms of the whole. In many cases, students do not even realize that there *is* a whole to be grasped.

A teaching model that focuses on topics that, in the student's mind, are disconnected from one another misses the crucial insight that *a field is itself a system of thinking*. A discipline has logic to it. It is not a set of discrete concepts, ideas, and procedures that can be fruitfully thought about in isolation from one another. To teach a discipline (or a field, or subject matter) is to teach students how to reason through the logic of the discipline, how to use that *system* of thinking (not just the individual parts) to analyze problems and situations.

How can this be done? It may require substantial reconstruction of a teacher's model of how to teach a discipline. It probably involves not allowing the logic of the textbook to dictate the logic of one's teaching. As a teacher, I can start by identifying for my students a small number—maybe just four or five, certainly no more than a dozen—of the most fundamental and powerful concepts, those that lie at the heart of thinking in the discipline. I can then identify two or three of the most central questions the course addresses. In the sociology course discussed earlier in this chapter, those fundamental and powerful concepts might include *social patterns* and *social forces;* the central questions might be, "What social patterns are evident in what people do?" and "What are the social forces that shape what people do?"

With these core concepts and questions articulated, I can then ask my students to do two things. First, they can work on how the fundamental and powerful concepts fit together to form a coherent system, and how the discipline tries to address its central questions. This is the work of critical thinking. It cannot be accomplished by having students sit and listen to the teacher's thinking. Critical thinking activities are valuable precisely because they are a way for students themselves to analyze and synthesize how a small group of concepts fit together as a logical system to make up the foundation of a discipline, or how those concepts fit in with the central questions.

Second, students can use the small group of concepts to think through a great variety of problems, ideas, situations, terms, events, states of affairs, and case studies. In fact, students use these concepts to think through virtually anything within the domain of the discipline. Notice that this range of problems can (and should) include those not explicitly addressed in the course, those lying in the student's life outside the classroom.

When taught accordingly, a sociology syllabus might read this way:

> This is a course in sociological thinking—thinking the way a sociologist thinks. As sociological thinkers, you will at all times be engaged in addressing two central questions: "How do people act and think in social groups?" and "Why do they act and think that way?" The two most fundamental concepts in the course are thus *social patterns* and *social forces.*
>
> Your textbook is one major resource for helping you improve your sociological thinking. At the beginning, we will work through several chapters together, using those two concepts as the foundation for understanding every single important topic. As the course progresses, you will be expected to take several chapters and think through them on your own using the same two concepts as the basis of your understanding.
>
> In addition, both in class and on exams, you will be expected to identify social patterns in people's behavior and explain that behavior in terms of social forces. The behavior to be explained usually includes examples that have not previously been addressed in class or in the text. Your responses will be assessed on the extent to which they are clear, accurate, relevant, and deep and give weight to alternative reasonable interpretations.

## Conclusion

Community college instruction, done well, lays a foundation for lifelong learning—for personal and professional life, for subsequent educational experience, and for participation in democracy. In the end, this can be accomplished only by teaching for critical thinking and by teaching for it in a way that is all-pervasive in classes, systematic within a discipline, and focused always on what is central and most transferable.

## References

Macionis, J. J. *Sociology* (8th ed.). Upper Saddle River, N.J.: Prentice Hall, 2001.
Paul, R., Elder, L., and Bartell, T. *California Teacher Preparation for Instruction in Critical Thinking: Research Findings and Policy Recommendations.* Sacramento: California Commission on Teacher Credentialing, 1997.

GERALD M. NOSICH *is professor of philosophy at the University of New Orleans.*

*Challenged by unconventional assignments, students examine untested assumptions and in the process become better critical thinkers.*

# Thwarting Expectations: Assignments from a Critical Thinking Class

*Jerry Herman*

> When I think back on all the crap I learned in high school, it's a wonder I can think at all.
> —Paul Simon, "Kodachrome"

Though the lyrics were written in the seventies, Paul Simon's words may ring truer now than then. College teachers despair at how ill-equipped first- and second-year community college students are to think on anything but the most superficial level. They may come from public high schools where the curriculum is dumbed down, where "creationism" is taught as equivalent to evolution, where *Catcher in the Rye* and *The Adventures of Huckleberry Finn* get censored, where classes are overcrowded, and textbooks outdated. Add to that mix poverty, illiteracy, a "fly speck" attention span, and it really is a wonder that they can think at all.

I teach at Laney College in Oakland, California, an urban community college whose student body is as diverse as any in the country. In the late 1980s, a critical thinking course became a requirement for transfer to a four-year school. When I volunteered to design and teach it, I had to take this diversity into account. This meant fashioning a one-size-fits-all curriculum with demanding standards that could not assume too much about students' prior learning and life experience.

After examining numerous books, I decided to use Marlys Mayfield's *Thinking for Yourself* (2003) because it includes fundamental topics such as observation, language, and facts that many other books do not, as well as more conventional subjects such as inference, opinion, argument, and fallacy. Mayfield's tone and language are well suited to our diverse population. The book proved effective, and I still use it.

But I went beyond the book in developing the new curriculum. Ordinarily students come into a class with assumptions and expectations—about the course, about education, and about themselves—few of which they have thoughtfully examined. Exposing and challenging unexamined assumptions and expectations seems to me a crucial element of critical thinking, so I decided to make subverting those assumptions a cornerstone of the course, a motif that would underpin whatever topic the class was considering.

This chapter describes three assignments in my critical thinking class that have proven to be effective in constructively subverting students' assumptions. However, this is not all that the assignments do. The first two, on observation and fact finding, have narrowly focused objectives. The third assignment, the group project, connects the dots between all the concepts and information covered during the semester and combines what might have appeared to be disparate parts into a unified whole.

## Critical Thinking Assignments

The following assignments are described in detail because each point has proven to be important for it to work optimally in my classes. However, colleagues who have used these assignments have adapted them to suit their own needs and tastes without loss of effectiveness.

**Produce.** Improving observation skills is an essential step toward critical thinking. If one is unable to record perceptions accurately, mentally or in writing, then the results will be skewed, no matter how skillfully one applies subsequent critical thinking. To develop observation skills, students in my classes observe a fruit or vegetable and describe it in a detailed essay. The key to this assignment lies in its requirements, which make some students gasp, some snicker, and others consider dropping the course:

> Choose a fruit or a vegetable. Devote at least one full hour to observing it closely and carefully, using your senses of sight, touch, hearing, taste, and smell. Be sure to give sufficient time to examining both the exterior and interior of the fruit or vegetable you observe. It's best to do your observation at one sitting.
>
> While you are observing the fruit or vegetable, monitor your thoughts and feelings during the process. Did you become excited, interested, frustrated, bored, impatient, or surprised? Note those thoughts and feelings and how they affect your observation.
>
> Write an essay in which you include these elements: a complete description of the fruit or vegetable, including the observations of all of your senses; a description of the thoughts and feelings you experienced during the observation; and two paragraphs of at least eight lines each discussing what you learned from doing this assignment.

The idea of devoting an hour to observing a piece of produce is—to say the least—novel to most students. A common reaction is that I'm crazy. What could be more boring and useless than looking at a piece of fruit, and how could it possibly take more than five minutes? I seem even crazier after I assure the students that they will find an hour not nearly enough time. They don't believe it, even though I tell them I have read thousands of essays saying just that.

Despite their skepticism, students complete the assignment after I guide them carefully through the steps. I read to the class excellent essays by former students. We discuss the need to be alone while observing (roommates make fun of you; children want to eat the fruit). I caution them to write only about the individual fruit or vegetable in front of them; this is not an assignment to research the history of pomegranates. We discuss vocabulary to describe the senses, and we conclude that smell and taste are the hardest to describe.

I am no longer astonished at the resulting essays. The overwhelming majority of them do say that an hour is not enough time for a detailed observation of their fruit or vegetable. Most students become so engrossed in observation that they lose track of time and are surprised to find that two hours have passed and they haven't even cut into the specimen yet. They find their observation unexpectedly fascinating. Many actually anthropomorphize their produce and give their tangerine or onion a name. They discover so much that is new and unexpected in such an everyday object that it opens their eyes to all they have been overlooking: "This assignment has taught me never to just look at something once and think that's all there is to it. After all, a peach isn't just an edible fruit; it's a whole other world waiting to be explored." They vow to be more cognizant and more appreciative of the details of the object. How much of this actually comes to pass, I don't know, but the very awareness of the need to be more observant is a vital first step to becoming a critical thinker.

**Finding Facts.** When my class reaches Mayfield's chapter on facts, we compare facts and certainties and discuss how facts change as the tools of human observation improve. It was once a fact that the earth was flat, that the sun revolved around the earth, and that the universe was static. But the invention of instruments such as the telescope consigned those supposed facts to the dustbin of history. We discuss how facts are ascertained; it is a revelation for many to realize that some facts are so fluid they are really only approximations (population figures, for example).

Moreover, when asked why they believe facts, most students respond that they don't believe anything they have not personally experienced. It's not difficult to disabuse them of that idea: "How many of you have been to New Zealand?" No hands go up. "How many believe that there is such a place as New Zealand?" All hands go up. "You believe that the existence of New Zealand is a fact, yet none of you has had the personal experience of having been there. It's likely that you believe there is such a place as New Zealand because you've heard about it or read it somewhere."

"How many of you believe that legal slavery existed in the United States before 1865?" All hands go up. "But none of you had the personal experience of being there either. As with your belief that New Zealand exists, you believe in historical facts because you've read or heard about them." Thus very quickly the class realizes that a scant few of the facts they believe have come from firsthand experience.

I follow this discussion with a practical exercise that demonstrates the difficulty of determining even seemingly simple facts. The classroom has moveable desks, randomly arranged. There are always more desks than students, some off in corners, although this is not evident to all students.

"Let's determine a simple fact," I say to a class of twenty to thirty students. "How many chairs are in this room? Let's stipulate that a chair is an object designed to be sat in, so the teacher's desk, for example, is not to be counted. Everyone count, and keep the final number to yourself."

When the buzz dies down and everyone has finished counting, I say, "On my count of three, everyone shout out your number; we should hear one number, called out in unison." But rather than a harmoniously expressed single number, there is a cacophony of numbers: "Thirty-nine!" "Forty-two!" "Forty-five!" "Forty-six!" "Forty-seven!" "Fifty-one!" (When I first started doing this exercise, I was apprehensive that everyone would come up with the same number, and the point would be lost. It has *never* happened.)

We discuss why the numbers are so varied and how to reach unanimity. Eventually the students establish a systematic way of counting, which usually takes the form of a designated student, with the entire class as witness, moving from chair to chair, touching each one, as he or she counts.

What is the effect of chair counting? It is striking for students to experience so personally the demonstration of what may seem like an abstract principle. As the semester progresses, the chair-counting lesson is often cited as an example of how very little should be taken for granted. Information and its sources should be scrutinized for accuracy and validity.

I follow chair counting with another major essay assignment, fact finding. Now aware that facts may not be easy to come by, students receive this assignment:

> When you get your fact to find, begin your search using problem-solving techniques. Stretch your imagination; write down strategies; ask everyone you think might be of help; don't shrink from doing something you might consider silly or embarrassing if it will help you in your quest. . . . You must get your fact from an authoritative source, and once you do so, verify it from at least one other authoritative source. If you find discrepancies between the two sources, you will have to reconcile them, perhaps by going to a third or fourth source.
>
> The essay assignment is to write a report (five hundred words minimum) that not only reports the facts you discovered but also describes the process

you went through, from the beginning to the point when you discovered and verified the facts you are to ascertain. . . . Include a section—at least two paragraphs of eight lines each—on what you learned from doing the assignment. Remember that the primary value in this project is in the process you go through to find your facts, not in the answers to the questions.

Over the years, I have developed a bank of questions that ask for facts that may be considered trivial but require resourcefulness and tenacity to answer and verify. Each student has his or her own fact(s) to find. There are no duplicates. One question, for example, asks: "What is the purpose of the weigh stations on California highways and freeways? What is their history? Who has jurisdiction over them?" Another inquires: "When, and under what circumstances, did the Catholic Church forbid abortion?" Other examples include: "How many footballs do all NFL teams use in a season? How many kinds (not manufacturers' brands) of footballs are there? Why?" "How many weather satellites are there? Who owns them? How do they work? How much does it cost to subscribe to their services?" "How many structures in the Bay Area did Julia Morgan design? In what cities are they located?"

Though I recognize the value of the Internet, I don't want students to get their answers there. It is too easy. To be valuable, this assignment must put forward a difficult challenge. If a student does find an answer on the Internet, I drop the question from future use. For most of the questions, the telephone is the students' most useful tool. They become investigative reporters. For most of them, it gives "research" a new meaning.

We spend much class time discussing strategies to complete the assignment. Fact finding can be frustrating because the answers to these questions are not typically in anyone's common range of knowledge, so they require arduous, frustrating pursuit. Students often hit a stone wall (e-mails not answered, voice-mail loops that preclude speaking with an actual person), but most of them do a conscientious job and eventually come up with the answers and verification. As critical thinkers, they have been required to solve a multifaceted problem and find fruitful new avenues for access to information.

**The Group Project.** The culmination of the semester, and the activity that synthesizes all the critical thinking skills developed so far, is the group project. Carrying a set of assumptions based on past experiences, students are wary of group projects. They grumble that the workload falls on one member of the group (oddly enough, always on the complaining party), that their grade will be lowered by less-adept students, and that they have to go through the gut-wrenching terror of making a formal presentation in front of their classmates. They claim that the presentations are never coordinated and early presenters hog the time, leaving little or no time for those at the end.

I honor each of these objections, yet I have refined the process over the years so that the only one that remains valid is the anxiety of making the class presentation—but even this is not a bad thing. I did not have much hope for the group project when I started it years ago, but when the first few were more successful than I expected, I continued with them, adjusting and modifying as needed. Today I consider this group project to be the most significant achievement of my forty-plus years of teaching.

The goal of the project is a well-researched, carefully thought-out, well-prepared hour-long presentation to the class on a topic of current interest:

> The purpose of these projects is to encourage you to use the knowledge and skills you have accumulated and practiced in this class by applying them systematically to familiar subjects that you may never have studied deeply before. The projects are being assigned to groups because the work involved is probably too great for an individual to do, but more important, you can learn more from collaborative work, especially in thinking. You benefit by observing how other people think and by working with them.
>
> You will be working in groups of four to six. Group members will find that careful organization and allotment of time and fair assignment of tasks work most effectively. Cooperation is essential for the group to come up with a unified and strong presentation.

The topics I choose may change from semester to semester, but I try to keep them challenging and relevant to students' interests. Here is a current list: contemporary slavery, current U.S. immigration, a close analysis of three or four television commercials, U.S. consumerism and its history, and analysis of consumer concerns regarding a particular product.

Students are quite concerned with how the groups are going to be formed. The key is to let the students choose their own groups according to their interest in the topic. A fatal flaw in many group projects is that students are assigned to groups by the instructor or by an arbitrary lottery system. The seeds of resentment, should anything go wrong with the group, will have already been sown.

About six weeks before the first presentation is scheduled, I distribute a detailed assignment sheet, which includes a lengthy description of each topic. I discuss them, and then let the students make their choices. Within less than fifteen minutes of negotiating voluntary switches if some groups are too small or large, the four groups of four to six students have been formed.

The groups meet at the end of this class session. After introductions and exchange of contact information, they get down to the business of how to proceed. Everything from scheduling meetings (probably the toughest problem to solve in a nonresidential college) to allotment of tasks, as well as researching, analyzing, and organizing the substantive material of their topic requires using the critical thinking skills the class has been building.

I allocate some class time to group meetings, but the groups get together primarily outside of class. During in-class meetings, I consult with each group, checking on progress, offering them resources, assuring myself they are on track, nudging them to move forward if I sense lack of movement. This monitoring-coaching function serves as an anchor for the groups. They do not drift off into inactivity if they know I am checking on them. They also know I am there to help if problems arise that they cannot solve.

I emphasize the necessity for discipline in preparing the presentation. I compare it to an athletic contest or a performance of any sort. One hour for the presentation is all each group gets. I accept no notes, no overtime, and no excuses. My evaluation of the group presentation is based exclusively on what the group does during that hour. Therefore, a careful proportional division of time for the presenters is vital, and rehearsals are essential for success.

During the weeks of putting the group project together, many students who seem to have nothing in common connect personally and intellectually. These connections are among the most valuable aspects of the project. Students learn to trust, respect, and rely on each other, eventually recognizing that genuine collaboration creates better results and is more personally satisfying than working in isolation. This is not to suggest that the path is smooth; far from it, but the lessons learned from surmounting the obstacles are invaluable. This passage from a student paper expresses the typical sentiment:

> I felt proud of each and every one of us, proud that we had all overcome what had been a significant psychological barrier to having to rely on other people to do work for which each individual would be held accountable; proud, too, of the tenacity we all exhibited in sticking with disciplined boundaries in order to tell one part of the story with great care. I love these people and really hope that this group project, which is now over, will be the beginning of an even longer project of friendship. With my friends in the group I have had the notion reinforced that education is an interactive process and that the most enduring lessons are learned together.

Virtually all of the presentations demonstrate how committed the groups have been. They show solid research, efficient organization, and well-thought-out conclusions about their topic. The general level of group achievement is significantly above the level of individual work in the class. Those students who were concerned about their grade being dragged down by others in the group have another of their assumptions subverted. Typically, more than 85 percent of students earn a grade for the group presentation that is higher than or equivalent to their prior grade average.

Do students experience performance anxiety? Of course. But the sense of triumph and self-confidence that follows a successful presentation makes it more than worthwhile: "Before the project was completed, I lacked confidence in myself and worried about what others would think of me. Now I feel more confident in myself than ever before, and I have come a long way in overcoming my fear of speaking in public. Overall this project has been a transforming experience." Another student wrote: "This semester I dropped Speech three weeks into the class because I knew I couldn't get up in front of an entire classroom of people, but it was too late to drop this class. I did it though. I talked for at least eight whole minutes—without puking and without passing out."

The final step in the group project is the individual report. A standard complaint about group projects is that it is not fair; some group members do more (or less) work than others, yet everyone gets the same grade. However, I worked out a compromise that not only satisfies the students but gives me the best feedback I can ask for about the project: the individual report.

The individual report is an essay recounting the student's contributions to the group, the group's progress, and what the student learned in the process. The individual reports allow me to differentiate among the work of individuals in the group and reward or penalize students accordingly. The grade for the individual report constitutes 35 percent of the grade for the project, while the presentation grade constitutes 65 percent.

The great critical thinking value of the individual report lies in requiring students to reflect on this major, six-week project. Rather than just putting the project out of their mind once the presentation has been made, students must think about it from a new perspective that adds depth and texture to the experience.

I get the benefit of a detailed description and analysis of how the groups worked. The points of view in each group give me a comprehensive picture of group dynamics and accomplishment. I make changes in the project on the basis of what I read, and I also feel gratified at the positive comments most of the students make. Once again, it is an assignment that constructively undercuts their expectations. One student closed his essay this way: "I'm glad that I have finally had a positive experience with group projects; it's a nice contrast to my past experiences. My research skills, which I consider my forte, were put to the test with this project, and at the end of the day I felt the others had matched me in efforts and skill. . . . The group assignment is definitively a culmination of prior instruction."

The three assignments described in this chapter represent a good portion of the semester's work in my critical thinking class. The remaining work is equally demanding, and I hope equally productive in developing my students' critical thinking skills, especially in making connections and examining assumptions. I remember one student who, for the first few weeks, slouched in his desk looking bored. One day he abruptly raised his hand. When I recognized him, he said somewhat indignantly, as though the light bulb had just flashed on, "I get it. You're not trying to teach us *things*. You're trying to change the way we think."

Amen.

## Reference

Mayfield, M. *Thinking for Yourself: Developing Critical Thinking Skills Through Reading and Writing* (6th ed.). Boston: Thomson Heinle, 2003.

*JERRY HERMAN teaches at Laney College in Oakland, California, where he pioneered development of a critical thinking curriculum in the English department.*

8

*This chapter describes the context, development, and fall 2004 implementation of the Year of Critical Thinking at Prince George's Community College, an effort to engage all full-time and adjunct faculty in teaching critical thinking in their classes.*

# The Year of Critical Thinking at Prince George's Community College: An Integrated Professional Development Program

*William P. Peirce*

For many years, Prince George's Community College (Maryland) has presented faculty development workshops on such pedagogical topics as learning styles, classroom assessment techniques, online teaching, reading strategies, journals, and critical thinking. Unfortunately, few of these workshops seem to have inspired wide-scale change in the institution. Some faculty feel they are already teaching critical thinking and do not need to do anything more. Others believe their primary obligation is to cover course content, not use class for time-consuming critical thinking activities. As well, adjunct faculty seldom attend these workshops.

Prince George's Community College (PGCC) is not alone in facing these difficulties. Research shows that although institutions of higher learning claim to value critical thinking, it is not being taught effectively. As Paul, Elder, and Bartell (1997) write, "Though the overwhelming majority [of faculty] (89%) claimed critical thinking to be a primary objective of their instruction . . . only 9 percent of the respondents were clearly teaching for critical thinking on a typical day in class" (p. 18).

Critical thinking is sorely needed in two-year college classrooms, however, because national assessments of community college students' ability to think critically reveal that they are not very good at it. They arrive from high school as weak critical thinkers, and they graduate from community college as weak critical thinkers. A national study (U.S. Department of Education,

2003) of high school seniors' persuasive writing skills revealed that more than two-thirds of seniors (69 percent) performed at a basic level or below, 22 percent were considered skillful, and only 9 percent were excellent.

Unfortunately, attending a community college does not appear to turn students into good critical thinkers. In 2004, 8,675 sophomores at fifty-one two-year colleges took the Educational Testing Service's Academic Profile test, which assesses general education competencies, including critical thinking. On the critical thinking portion of the test, 86 percent of students were considered not proficient, 11 percent were considered marginal, and only 3 percent were considered proficient. That is, 97 percent of two-year college sophomores could not perform such critical thinking tasks as evaluating competing causal explanations and determining the relevance of information for evaluating an argument or conclusion (Educational Testing Service, 2004).

Despite nineteen years of faculty development workshops promoting Writing and Reasoning Across the Curriculum concepts, PGCC students' critical thinking scores on the Academic Profile test show the same weaknesses revealed in the national scores. Recognizing this fact, PGCC launched the Year of Critical Thinking, an effort to involve all of PGCC's 250 full-time and 500 adjunct faculty in improving the teaching of critical thinking. PGCC also created the Critical Thinking Institute, through which liaisons from each department meet once a month to discuss ways of involving more of their departmental faculty in teaching thinking, and to consider revising courses to include explicit teaching of thinking. This chapter describes the context, development, and fall 2004 implementation of the Year of Critical Thinking at Prince George's Community College, and presents details about each component.

## The Year of Critical Thinking at PGCC

Planning for the Year of Critical Thinking at PGCC began in fall 2003, when the vice president of instruction convened a task force to brainstorm how to engage all faculty—especially adjuncts—in emphasizing critical thinking in their courses. The task force consisted of faculty involved in professional development at the college, notably the coordinator of the Center for Teaching and Learning; the director of the Writing Center; and the coordinators of Writing Across the Curriculum, Reasoning Across the Curriculum, and Communication Across the Curriculum. We called ourselves the Think Tank and met once or twice a month to think creatively about how to change faculty attitudes and practices, and how to reach beyond those professors already committed to critical thinking.

The college's approach to critical thinking was always to encourage faculty to infuse critical thinking across the curriculum, rather than require a single course in critical thinking. The Think Tank recommended continuing the faculty development model and emphasized a broad definition of critical thinking, one that encompassed good disciplinary thinking in place of emphasizing only formal and informal logic.

Since the college already had a history of faculty workshops that encouraged critical thinking, the phrase "critical thinking initiative" (which suggested a new emphasis) was abandoned, and instead we began to call our fall 2004 adventure "the Year of Critical Thinking" (suggesting that critical thinking is something to focus on now).

The goal of the Year of Critical Thinking is to enhance faculty development in order to engage all full-time and adjunct faculty in working to improve the teaching of critical thinking across the curriculum. Eventually, we hope the Year of Critical Thinking will help students strengthen their thinking about their coursework; demonstrate sound thinking on tests, assignments, and class projects; transfer critical thinking skills from one course to another; and have the strategic, analytical, problem-solving, and decision-making skills they will need when they transfer to another college or join the workforce.

## PGCC's Definition of Critical Thinking

PGCC's understanding of critical thinking is modeled after definitions proposed by the Foundation for Critical Thinking (Scriven and Paul, 2004) and is defined as the sound thinking within a discipline that is needed and relied upon by practitioners in that discipline—thinking that is accurate, relevant, reasonable, and rigorous, whether it be analyzing, synthesizing, generalizing, applying concepts, interpreting, evaluating, supporting arguments and hypotheses, solving problems, or making decisions. Applying critical thinking in the classroom should consist of teaching students to find answers, solve problems, and make decisions in the same way practitioners in the discipline do. This definition assumes that learning, applying, and thinking about factual content are interdependent processes.

## Major Features of the Year of Critical Thinking

The Year of Critical Thinking involves both professional development activities previously in place at PGCC as well as some new ones. In the past, PGCC usually had a fall keynote speaker, an October College Enrichment Day, professional development workshops, and a Web site with resources for teaching critical thinking. During the Year of Critical Thinking, all of these activities focus on teaching thinking. In addition to these familiar activities, there are such new creations as the Critical Thinking Institute, a handbook of resources and examples, and an April "best practices" conference. These components are described in detail in this section and can be modified to accommodate the unique needs and circumstances of other community colleges.

**Keynote Speaker.** As in most community colleges, faculty return to campus the week before classes start for five days of meetings and workshops.

In fall 2004, the keynote address was delivered by Rosemary R. Haggett, of the National Science Foundation, whose address on "What It Means to be Educated in the Twenty-First Century" emphasized the need for sound critical and disciplinary thinking. Although Haggett was invited independently of the Year of Critical Thinking, her presentation enhanced the focus on critical thinking for the ensuing year. Having a keynote speaker who highlighted the need for teaching critical thinking and presented classroom strategies helped motivate faculty to get involved in the activities that would be presented later in the year.

**Critical Thinking Institute.** The Critical Thinking Institute is the heart of the PGCC's critical thinking program and is the chief difference between the college's previous faculty development initiatives and the Year of Critical Thinking. Until 2004, PGCC's usual method of professional development was to ask various faculty members and committees to present workshops with appealing descriptions to whomever showed up. These workshops were offered regularly throughout the year. Typically, fewer than 10 percent of full-time faculty attended the individual workshop sessions, and rarely did more than two or three adjunct faculty attend. We have high hopes that the Critical Thinking Institute will be an agent of change and renewal among a large number of our faculty—especially adjuncts.

The Critical Thinking Institute consists of twenty-four faculty members who meet once a month, and it is led by a coordinator who has release time. A faculty member from each of PGCC's twenty-four academic departments, ideally one who is already an experienced practitioner of active learning strategies, was appointed by his or her department chair to be its liaison to the Critical Thinking Institute. The liaisons are leading their departments in examining the parts of their courses that already teach critical thinking well, and the parts that need strengthening.

For example, some liaisons are leading their departments in revising multiple-choice tests to include a greater number of higher-order thinking questions; another liaison is designing critical reading activities for an introductory first-year writing course. One department already includes explicit critical thinking outcomes and activities in their introductory course and is developing an assessment to see if students actually learn those objectives. The department will also assess the same outcomes at the beginning of the next course their students take to see if the skills have been transferred. Our hope is that a great many classroom activities, assignments, projects, and departmental discussions will develop from these dialogues.

**Facultywide Workshops on Strategies for Teaching Critical Thinking.** As coordinator of PGCC's Reasoning Across the Curriculum program, I already do and will continue to present collegewide workshops on such topics as improving students' meta-cognitive abilities and strategies for teaching thinking in online classes. If asked by the departmental liaisons in the Critical Thinking Institute, I will also conduct workshops tailored for individual departments.

**Workshops on Critical Thinking on College Enrichment Day.** Each October, PGCC suspends classes and office work for a day so that the entire faculty and staff can attend workshops and meetings on a variety of topics that enrich their professional work. In October 2004, Barbara J. Millis, coauthor of *Cooperative Learning for Higher Education Faculty* (Millis and Cottell, 1998), presented three well-attended (and well-received) workshops for faculty on using cooperative learning strategies to improve students' critical thinking. The evening workshop of College Enrichment Day was designed especially for adjunct faculty. Bringing in outside experts to conduct workshops not only brought new strategies and resources to the faculty but also demonstrated the college's commitment to the Year of Critical Thinking.

**Online Critical Thinking Course for Faculty.** In addition to the other components of PGCC's Year of Critical Thinking, one of the college's philosophy professors is offering faculty a self-paced online course in critical thinking. She created the course by selecting elements of two courses in formal logic and critical thinking that are usually offered to students, and tailoring it to the faculty. The college contributes $55 to each professor or staff member who enrolls in the course to defray the cost of the textbook. Thus far, twenty-six faculty and administrators have enrolled in the course.

The online course presents a common understanding of critical reasoning concepts and classroom applications; Part One was offered in fall 2004, and Part Two will be offered in spring 2005. Part One begins with an introduction to basic concepts: critical reasoning as deduction and induction, validity, soundness, strength and cogency of arguments, and techniques to prove the invalidity of an argument. Next, a module on language, meaning, and definition prepares participants for detailed study of informal fallacies. Part Two focuses, for the most part, on inductive reasoning, covering topics such as the role analogy plays in legal and moral reasoning, techniques for determining causality, and understanding statistics as evidence.

In both parts, faculty write projects showing how they use and evaluate critical reasoning in class. For example, an accounting professor plans to have students use Venn diagrams, and a music professor is designing assignments for composition students that distill critical and intuitive elements in composing. Thomson Learning, the publisher of the textbook used in the course, is planning to set up a Web site with PGCC's class projects as a pilot to demonstrate pedagogical applications of the textbook material. Thomson Learning has also invited the PGCC faculty to write a book on pedagogical applications of critical thinking and logic concepts.

**Handbook of Critical Thinking Resources.** PGCC's handbook of critical thinking resources includes sample assignments in several disciplines, lists of resources, and brief articles on teaching strategies that promote critical thinking, critical reading, and information literacy. It was distributed to all full-time and adjunct faculty at the start of the Year of Critical Thinking; along with other resources for teaching critical thinking, it is available online.

**Online Resources for Teaching Critical Thinking.** PGCC's Reasoning Across the Curriculum Web site (http://academic.pgcc.edu/~wpeirce/MCCCTR) contains articles with teaching strategies, workshop handouts, lists of books on teaching thinking, links to other Web sites on teaching thinking, a list of URLs for students writing persuasive arguments, and so forth. For the Year of Critical Thinking, it received a modest face-lift, and several articles were updated.

**Conference Showcasing Best Practices by PGCC Faculty.** In April 2005, PGCC expects to host an in-house conference publicizing the best classroom activities, assignments, and projects that have developed out of the departmental dialogues inspired by the Critical Thinking Institute. Examples of what works for one teacher might inspire teachers in other disciplines to design their own variations of the assignment or classroom activity. The college plans to make the next critical thinking conference a regional event.

## Cost of the Year of Critical Thinking

The Year of Critical Thinking is cost-effective. Two faculty, the coordinator of the Reasoning Across the Curriculum program and the coordinator of the Critical Thinking Institute, have received release time to serve as co-coordinators of the Year of Critical Thinking. In addition, the two outside speakers are paid a modest stipend. Other costs include in-house printing for the handbook, flyers, and posters, and money for refreshments at the spring conference. Finally, the college gave each faculty member who enrolled in the online course $55 to help pay for the textbook.

## Conclusion

Since I am finishing this chapter in January, one semester after PGCC launched the Year of Critical Thinking program, I cannot yet report on how well it worked. The Office of Planning and Institutional Research is designing a survey to be administered in spring 2005 to assess faculty satisfaction with the program, solicit suggestions for the following year, and inquire whether the Year of Critical Thinking actually resulted in changes in faculty members' courses.

As well, although this is not the specific focus of the Year of Critical Thinking, we hope that students' critical thinking scores on the Academic Profile test will increase over time. The ultimate goal of PGCC's Year of Critical Thinking is to increase the number of full-time and adjunct faculty who (to echo the words of Paul, Elder, and Bartell) are "clearly teaching for critical thinking on a typical day in class" (1997, p. 18).

# References

Educational Testing Service. "Academic Profile Comparative Data." Washington, D.C.: Educational Testing Service. http://www.ets.org/hea/acpro/compare.html. Accessed Aug. 25, 2004.

Millis, B. J., and Cottell, P. G. *Cooperative Learning for Higher Education Faculty.* Phoenix, Ariz.: American Council on Education/Oryx Press, 1998.

Paul, R., Elder, L., and Bartell, T. *California Teacher Preparation for Instruction in Critical Thinking: Research Findings and Policy Recommendations.* Sacramento: California Commission on Teacher Credentialing, 1997.

Scriven, M., and Paul, R. "Defining Critical Thinking: A Statement for the National Council for Excellence in Critical Thinking Instruction." Dillon Beach, Calif.: Foundation for Critical Thinking, 2004. http://www.criticalthinking.org/aboutCT/definingCT.shtml. Accessed Dec. 3, 2004.

U.S. Department of Education, National Center for Education Statistics. "The Nation's Report Card: Writing 2002." Washington D.C.: U.S. Department of Education, 2003. http://nces.ed.gov/pubsearch/pubsinfo.asp?pubid=2003529. Accessed Feb. 15, 2005.

*WILLIAM P. PEIRCE is professor of English and coordinator of Reasoning Across the Curriculum at Prince George's Community College in Largo, Maryland.*

*Critical Literacy, a special approach to teaching critical thinking, has survived and thrived at Montgomery College in the face of a shifting political and pedagogical climate, thanks to programmatic adaptability and alertness to opportunities.*

# The Evolution of Critical Literacy at Montgomery College

*Francine M. Jamin, Marcia Bronstein*

Fifteen years ago, Montgomery College, Maryland's oldest and largest community college, launched its Critical Literacy movement, a special approach to critical thinking that was adapted from a model originally developed at Oakton Community College (Illinois). At Montgomery, Critical Literacy is defined as a set of skills and dispositions that promote creative teaching and active learning across the curriculum. The term is relatively new, but the concept is basic to all good pedagogy. For college students, Critical Literacy is the ability to read with comprehension, think critically about course content, write in a manner appropriate to specific disciplines, and become actively engaged in learning. For college faculty, Critical Literacy offers a fresh perspective on the processes of teaching and learning, as well as methods for assessing whether learning has occurred.

Throughout its existence at Montgomery College, Critical Literacy has experienced periods of buoyant expansion and sobering retrenchment. Ultimately however, despite changes in college and federal administrations, budgetary boom and bust, and shifting institutional priorities, Critical

Critical thinking luminaries who left their imprint on Montgomery College's fledgling program include Richard Paul, John Chaffee, Vincent Ruggiero, and Stephen Brookfield. In addition, we are indebted to Lynda Jerit, of Oakton Community College, for the concept of "crash-and-burn sites" and the need to anticipate and address them. We also remain indebted to our other Oakton mentors: Lorenz Boehm, Marilee McGowan, Alan Rubin, and William Taylor. Finally, Christine McMahon, guest editor of this volume, was the founding coordinator of Critical Literacy, and for many years she provided leadership and inspiration for the critical thinking movement at Montgomery College.

Literacy has not only survived but actually experienced several distinctive rebirths. We attribute this longevity to programmatic adaptability in the face of a shifting political and pedagogical climate. Granted, there were some serendipitous occurrences, but we also made our own good luck by being alert to opportunities and ready to capitalize on them. This chapter reflects on the evolution of the Critical Literacy movement at Montgomery College, which occurred in three distinct stages.

## 1990–1997: Creation and Expansion

In 1990, Montgomery's collegewide Writing Across the Curriculum committee, active since 1984, undertook serious self-scrutiny. The group had made substantial progress enlisting the support of colleagues from non-humanities disciplines, and periodic expert presentations on assignment design and learning assessment were well attended. Yet few original ideas were forthcoming, and even allies in the disciplines were struggling to assign and assess writing while adequately covering the mandated course content. In short, the program needed a new direction and an infusion of energy.

One suggestion was to take a closer look at the new critical thinking pedagogy. In particular, the techniques of meta-cognition—the rigorous monitoring of thought processes based on explicit criteria advocated by Richard Paul and others—held promise for those seeking to develop and enforce curriculumwide standards of effective communication.

Although its underlying principles were not new, critical thinking and its logical outgrowth of Socratic teaching based on adept questioning were beginning to command renewed attention in educational circles in the mid- to late-1980s. The impact of this rediscovered pedagogy was especially powerful at the community college, where classroom teaching is the most honored vocation and where professors—who are theorists as well as practitioners of their craft—constantly seek out ways to help their students learn how to learn.

At this time, Oakton Community College, which already had a thriving critical thinking program, was awarded an AACJC/Kellogg Beacon College grant to introduce the "new" pedagogy to community college faculty across the country. A team of three faculty members and one administrator from Montgomery College, along with nine other community college teams, were selected to participate in a weeklong onsite institute at Oakton in January 1992.

During this training, we absorbed critical thinking theory and related it to practical pedagogy. We began by formulating alternative definitions of critical thinking and then examined those definitions critically. Focusing on a class that we taught regularly, each of us drew a course "map," analyzing the shape and progression of a semester, and identifying the "crash-and-burn sites"—points at which things predictably go wrong.

To create a theoretical underpinning for practical pedagogy, we reviewed Bloom's taxonomy (1956) of lower-order (knowledge, comprehension, application) and higher-order (analysis, synthesis, evaluation) thinking skills. Bloom's hierarchy of cognitive skills reinforced the need for logical progression and cumulative build in our lesson plans. A review of William Perry's research on stages of cognitive development (1970)—in which students move from dualism through multiplicity to relativism and finally to commitment within relativism—added the insight that mastery of higher-order thinking skills depends in part on developmental readiness. We also considered the influence of gender variables and paid specific attention to "women's ways of knowing" (Belenky, Clinchy, Goldberger, and Tarule, 1986). Finally, we role-played scenarios for employing specific classroom practices such as full-group discussion and collaborative learning.

Not surprisingly, we returned from Oakton radiating enthusiasm for the new pedagogy to which we had been exposed, and this experience greatly influenced the shaping of Montgomery College's own Critical Literacy movement. At this point, the Writing Across the Curriculum committee voted to transform itself into a group focused on critical thinking. In adopting the Critical Literacy designation, we also signed on to Oakton's underlying pedagogy: to fuse instruction in critical thinking skills and dispositions with the teaching of communication skills and information literacy; to teach students to think critically not by approaching them directly but by creating a powerful faculty development initiative; and to ask faculty to become mentors and role models for students.

To colleagues who feared we were fomenting a pedagogical revolution, we responded that Montgomery College's Critical Literacy movement would encourage all faculty to build on what they already did well, to explore new areas if so inclined, and to share their experiences and insights with colleagues.

We also committed ourselves more broadly to investigating learning theories and developing classroom practices that enhance critical thinking. Taking advantage of the fact that community college faculty get to teach certain introductory courses repeatedly, we experimented with the design of those courses, striving for the most effective sequencing of lessons and assignments. Teaching at a college whose students represent more than 170 countries, we reflected on how ethnic, racial, and gender variables might influence teaching and learning. Even though we had long recognized a variety of student learning styles, we now came to realize that there was a similarly broad range of preferred teaching styles. For example, we all agreed that lecture by itself is an ineffective way of engaging students. Yet we differed in our approaches to interactive or collaborative learning; some of us preferred small peer-group tasks, while others found full-group discussion more effective.

Thus, our background in critical thinking pedagogy gave us a set of terms and concepts by which to analyze and critique our own classroom practice. We fell in love with teaching all over again, feeling intellectually curious rather than disheartened when a class went badly. Working from our new theoretical framework, we could engage in meta-cognitive self-scrutiny, asking, for instance, precisely what went wrong in that terrible class this morning? At what point did things start to deteriorate? Could the problem have been anticipated and avoided? Might the lesson have been taught more effectively in another way or at another point in the semester? Then there was the exhilaration of going back to the classroom (our laboratory) and trying again in a different way.

Generously funded by a supportive administration during the economic boom of the 1990s, we had the luxury of launching our enterprise with a year of planning. Under the able leadership of Christine McMahon, our first Critical Literacy coordinator, and with input from faculty and lead administrators, we devised a comprehensive plan for the next five years. Its centerpiece was a series of biweekly faculty seminars for which twelve participants each academic year would receive three hours of release time from teaching per semester. We developed a schedule of seminar sessions modeled after Oakton's, relying heavily on expert guest presenters since we had not yet identified our own areas of expertise. These guests included several of our Oakton mentors, as well as faculty from nearby colleges and universities who had been in the critical thinking business longer than we had.

Other features of our long-range plan included faculty-to-faculty mentoring, sponsorship of a regional Cherry Blossom conference on critical thinking each April, and establishment of a "consultancy center" to serve as a resource to other colleges and the community at large.

When we put out a call for applicants for the first round of faculty seminars, we were inundated with applications despite the seminars' rigorous demands (faculty were asked to attend sixteen biweekly sessions, complete substantial reading assignments for most sessions, keep a response journal, devise an individual project based on revision of a regularly taught course, submit a final report and portfolio, and offer a presentation to the full college faculty at the end of the academic year). Applications for that first "class" were then evaluated competitively, and the top candidates were chosen to be Critical Literacy "fellows."

When it came time to plan for a second seminar year, we discovered that we had begun to develop our own areas of specialization within critical thinking pedagogy and thus required fewer guest presenters. By the third year, we felt confident enough to mount the whole series ourselves.

For the first three years, success built upon success, and our program was lauded and emulated throughout the college. Then problems began to surface. As it turned out, in wholeheartedly embracing Oakton's Critical Literacy paradigm of faculty development we had inherited both its considerable strengths as well as some inherent vulnerabilities.

## 1997–2003: Consolidation and Retrenchment

In the late 1990s, money gradually became tighter as Montgomery County and the state of Maryland began to limit funding for higher education. Montgomery College officials, anticipating even tougher economic times, began to allocate resources more sparingly. Thus funding to purchase release time for faculty participants in Critical Literacy seminars was no longer readily available and had to be argued for and justified in each budget cycle. Mounting the seminars also became more problematic because fewer people were applying; we had, in effect, largely exhausted the pool of interested colleagues and the college was hiring fewer new and replacement faculty. Eventually, the Cherry Blossom conference, which ran for three glorious years and two lean ones, succumbed to similar pressures. The proposed consultancy center never made it past the drawing board.

In one unforeseen way, Montgomery College's Critical Literacy program gained wider visibility during this period of retrenchment. The purchase of computers for all Montgomery College faculty offices meant that e-mail was now readily available. It was at this time that the Critical Literacy Online Newsletter (CLON) began to appear about once a month. Originally conceived as a bulletin board for event notices and similar announcements, over the five years of its existence CLON became a forum for consideration of pedagogical issues and a publishing outlet for short think pieces on a range of subjects relating to cognitive theory and practical pedagogy. Distribution was by subscription only, and no advertising or promotion was ever done, yet nearly two hundred people at Montgomery College, across the country, and around the world subscribed. Eventually, however, as prospects for Critical Literacy darkened further CLON began to appear less frequently and eventually ceased publication.

On a chilly spring day in 1997, a group of Critical Literacy leaders sat dispiritedly at a picnic table on campus, trying to envision a viable future for the movement. They were haunted by the sense that the faculty development seminars had ended before the pedagogy they were promoting and modeling was truly established at the college. Refusing to accept a quiet demise, the group envisioned a bold new project that reached directly into the classroom and out to the community at large. Called Community Conversations, it became the centerpiece of Critical Literacy's efforts for the next six years.

Community Conversations engaged faculty and students across the three campuses of Montgomery College and within several county high schools in a sustained, informed discussion of important social problems, ones for which there were no ready answers. Multidisciplinary by necessity, Community Conversations was a yearly learning community of one hundred to two hundred students that linked participants in the study of a powerful theme through shared readings and writing assignments, online discussion, conversation with expert presenters, and a culminating communal discussion at a televised "town meeting" each spring.

During this time, fall semesters were devoted to faculty development. A group of five or more Montgomery College faculty and several high school teachers from diverse disciplines collaborated to create materials that would present the multiple dimensions of a significant social issue to their classes. Slowly, teachable questions were forged that could drive students' study in the spring semester, while accessible multidisciplinary readings were chosen and writing assignments created that students in all participating classes could share.

Community Conversations faculty development was practical, project-oriented, and content-based—hence different from the global, skills-based professional development of the previous years' Critical Literacy seminars. This sustained thematic inquiry, in which faculty interacted with each other across disciplinary borders and engaged in dialogue with national authorities, brought a strong sense of renewal to its participants. Sustained inquiry on a single theme was, in fact, the hallmark of Community Conversations.

Over its six-year run, Community Conversations earned praise within the college and the community and compiled an impressive record of achievement. It engaged fifty-some faculty and more than seven hundred students in intensive study and dialogue, attracted nationally recognized presenters, and never flinched from potentially confrontational issues. Serendipity (or foresight!) resulted in a selection of topics that reflected headline news and evoked keen local interest. The first town meeting on the roots of violence, whose planning had begun six months earlier, occurred the week after the school shootings at Columbine High School. The second town meeting, on the ethics of gene therapy, immediately preceded the stem cell debate. A sociolinguistic focus in the last two years of Community Conversations targeted political rhetoric in the aftermath of September 11, 2001.

Eventually, however, sustaining such an ambitious project on a very slim budget proved exhausting. At the same time, as official learning communities became institutionalized at Montgomery College, they largely obviated the need for the ad hoc design of Community Conversations. Ultimately, there was simply insufficient energy to revive Community Conversations year after year. Thus, with diminished energy within its ranks, and with administrative support and funding for its centerpiece initiative wavering, Critical Literacy once again faced an uncertain future at Montgomery College.

## 2003-Present: Serendipity and New Beginnings

In September 2003, Paul Peck, a local entrepreneur and philanthropist who had previously been a generous donor to Montgomery College, approached the college once again. His immediate concern, expressed in a letter to the executive vice president for academic and student services, was "the accelerating declines in voting, political civility, and civic participation that threaten our children's future." He attributed much of the problem to the fact that courses in civics, American history, and American culture were being deemphasized in the schools. In his words, "Our young people (our future) are not being prepared to fill their citizenship roles; and our country cannot maintain its freedom and greatness if Americans do not understand what their country stands for and how it works."

Having articulated this problem, Peck proposed a solution. He envisioned an organizational structure that would provide strong leadership in educating "Americans of all ages about our country, our history, our principles, and our responsibilities . . . to get more people participating in the civic and political process." To this end, he offered to establish a new institute at Montgomery College, the Paul Peck Institute for American Culture and Civic Engagement.

As coordinator of the Critical Literacy program, I (Francine Jamin) was chosen as director. In accepting this position, I realized there was a place under the new institute's umbrella for a revitalized Critical Literacy movement. After all, an informed and involved citizenry, as Paul Peck envisioned, would need training not only in history and politics but also in reasoning skills.

The institute's first project, the "Jefferson Café," has been extremely successful and has dovetailed perfectly with Critical Literacy methods and objectives. Its model is Socratic, in that it fosters a conversation that proceeds through questioning. Since the Paul Peck Institute focuses on American themes and questions about the role of the United States in the global community, the Cafés are named after Thomas Jefferson—one of our most intellectual presidents, a devotee of stimulating conversation, a man far enough back in time to avoid partisan identification, and an individual whose own life story raises many provocative questions.

The Jefferson Café comprises a small but diverse circle of roughly fifteen preregistered participants, including an ever-varying group of Montgomery College faculty, staff, administrators, and students, as well as a number of community members. Each monthly gathering includes both new and returning participants. We deliberately limit the number so that people can see and hear each other as they sit around a conference table. Each Jefferson Café takes off from a short reading on an agreed-upon topic, distributed to participants several weeks in advance. The text may turn out to be central to the discussion or serve as a launching point for consideration of related issues. There is no presenter, but a facilitator offers leading questions and otherwise unobtrusively guides the conversation.

One index of success is that all Cafés have been fully enrolled, and most have had a waiting list. Cafés on campus have spawned other Café series, and in July 2004, in the seventh month of the institute's existence, we initiated Cafés in community centers, senior centers, public libraries, art galleries, and other sites around the county. The following month, the institute was awarded a By the People grant from PBS-MacNeil/Lehrer Productions to recognize and support its Jefferson Café initiative.

This immediate success, on campus and in the community, demonstrates that there is a true hunger for critical reading and thoughtful, open-ended, civil conversation about ideas. Ultimately, from the momentum born of Café discussions, we hope to devise the framework for more open and inclusive Community Conversations. Perhaps we may also fulfill the dream of a community-oriented consultancy center that has so long eluded us.

A number of other programs sponsored by the Paul Peck Institute for American Culture and Civic Engagement also work to promote critical thinking. During the 2004 presidential campaign, the institute worked closely with the League of Women Voters of Montgomery County and other civic groups not only to register students eligible to vote but also to get them to think about complex issues confronting their community and their country. Working with the college's Center for Community Leadership Development and Public Policy and the offices of student life at Montgomery's three campuses, we cosponsored DebateWatch, an event that included viewing a presidential debate and a facilitated dialogue about candidates and issues. We also cosponsored public forums on the Montgomery County ballot questions. In keeping with the institute's slogan ("Be informed. Get involved"), we continue to challenge citizens to exercise their rights and embrace their responsibilities.

The institute's newly constructed Web site (http://www.montgomery college.edu/departments/americanculture) is yet another avenue for thoughtful networking. The site now includes a link to "Critical Thinking and Civic Engagement," thus furnishing a locus for the rebirth of the Critical Literacy Online Newsletter, this time with far greater visibility and accessibility.

Always, however, there is a cost. Under the institute's banner, Montgomery College's special brand of critical thinking pedagogy loses some name recognition and programmatic autonomy. For example, although the Critical Literacy designation is revered for historical reasons among the small group of founders, for our current purposes the term *critical thinking* has greater resonance. As well, although virtually every new project at the college includes in its mission statement a pledge of allegiance to critical thinking principles, beyond the institute no single body monitors the integrity of these claims. Gone are the days when Critical Literacy was a freestanding faculty development initiative.

From our point of view, however, the signs are hopeful. As a result of its affiliation with the Paul Peck Institute for American Culture and Civic Engagement, which has a high profile and is well funded, critical thinking has gained a new foothold within Montgomery College and the neighboring community. Each week brings new inquiries about our programs, as well as proposals for affiliated initiatives. We are regularly written up in local papers and have become sought-after guests on television programs. Over time and in the face of change and challenge, critical thinking has proved its viability at Montgomery College, and its current prospects look especially favorable.

## References

Belenky, M. F., Clinchy, B. M., Goldberger, N. R., and Tarule, J. M. *Women's Ways of Knowing: The Development of Self, Voice, and Mind.* New York: Basic Books, 1986.

Bloom, B. S. *Taxonomy of Educational Objectives: The Classification of Educational Goals: Handbook I, Cognitive Domain.* Reading, Mass.: Longman, 1956.

Perry Jr., W. G. *Forms of Intellectual and Ethical Development in the College Years: A Scheme.* Austin, Tex.: Holt, Rinehart and Winston, 1970.

*FRANCINE M. JAMIN, professor of English at Montgomery College, served for eight years as Critical Literacy coordinator; she is now director of the Paul Peck Institute for American Culture and Civic Engagement at Montgomery College.*

*MARCIA BRONSTEIN, professor of English at Montgomery College, was the originator of the Community Conversations project and its coordinator for several years; she now coordinates Interdisciplinary Studies at Montgomery College.*

10

*This chapter contains relevant information and resources about critical thinking for community college faculty, staff, and administrators who endeavor to implement new or strengthen existing critical thinking capabilities on their campus.*

# Critical Thinking Sources and Information for Community College Educators

*Shannon M. Calderone*

> Thinking is the method of an educative experience.
> —John Dewey

Although foundational to educational practice, the methods by which effectual development of thought is both supported and sustained on community college campuses remain a substantial challenge for students, faculty, and administrators. As the chapters in this volume have demonstrated, it can be challenging to implement critical thinking as an epistemology, a pedagogical practice, and an organizing principle for institutions of higher learning. Yet, as these chapters also demonstrate, improved understanding of critical thinking offers a context in which institutions can use their creative assets toward enhancing campuswide learning.

What is known, and articulated throughout this volume, is that critical thinking is more than a meta-cognitive task. It also involves careful cultivation of a host of motivational traits that serve to enhance our reflective capacities, improve our problem-solving skills, and foster "purposeful, self-regulatory judgment" (Facione, 1990, p. 2). Moreover, the development of such skills is not relegated to the classroom but ideally should be inculcated in all facets of institutional life (Tsui, 2000).

Our nation's community colleges are both historically and functionally situated to actuate innovative pedagogies that serve to enhance their students' critical thinking skills. As an important provider of college preparatory skills and vocational and technical education, as well as professional development and lifelong educational opportunity, community colleges are compelled to engage in purposeful practices that give students from all walks of life appropriate strategies for tackling the complexities of the modern work environment (Hirose, 1992).

To assist community college faculty, staff, and administrators as they endeavor to implement new or strengthen existing critical thinking capabilities on their campus, this chapter presents relevant information and resources about critical thinking. The majority of the resources highlighted in this chapter are available through the ERIC database at http://www.eric.ed.gov/. Consistent with the topics covered in this volume, this chapter offers suggestions for further reading on pedagogical strategies that support critical thinking in the college classroom, tools for assessing critical thinking skills, and information on applying critical thinking from an organizational or institutional perspective.

## Pedagogical Strategies That Support Critical Thinking

There are a number of resources designed to assist community college faculty and administrators in implementing critical thinking strategies in the classroom. The resources given here highlight some proven strategies for fostering critical engagement within the community college classroom.

National University of Singapore Critical Thinking and Pedagogy (http://www.cdtl.nus.edu.sg/ctp/index.htm)
    This Web site provides useful resources on incorporating critical thinking into pedagogy. In addition to a helpful glossary of critical thinking terminology and concepts, the site also offers a host of critical thinking exercises that serve to enhance reflective thinking, as well as inferential, deductive, and problem-solving skills within the classroom.

Kitchener, K. S., and King, P. M. "The Reflective Judgment Model: Ten Years of Research." In M. L. Commons, C. Armon, L. Kohnberg, F. A. Richards, T. A. Grotzer, and J. Sinnott (eds.), *Beyond Formal Operations III: Models and Methods in the Study of Adolescent and Adult Thought.* New York: Praeger, 1984.
    Kitchener and King offer a seven-stage model for developing reflective judgment that incorporates Piaget's notion of formal operations. The chapter also describes how reflective judgment should be identified, charts the progression of stages in which a person may be located, and gives a synthesis of existing research on the model.

Peirce, W. P. "Strategies for Teaching Thinking and Promoting Intellectual Development in Online Classes." In S. Reisman (ed.), *Electronic Communities: Current Issues and Best Practices.* Greenwich, Conn.: U.S. Distance Learning Association and Information Age Publishing, 2003.

This chapter highlights practical teaching strategies for enhancing critical thinking that can be used in online or distance learning settings. Particular focus is given to how teachers can overcome the challenges of asynchronous learning (two-way communication that involves a time delay between transmission and receipt), which often serve to undermine student engagement in course content. This discussion highlights the importance of using active learning strategies in encouraging good thinking skills, as well as the transformative capacity of online delivery systems en route to supporting students' intellectual development.

Brown, N. M., Freeman, K. E., and Williamson, C. L. "The Importance of Critical Thinking for Student Use of the Internet." *College Student Journal,* 2000, 34(3), 391–398.

Research indicates that the Internet now serves as a primary research venue for community college students (Bower and Hardy, 2004). Easy access and a relative wealth of information make the Web an attractive researching tool. Yet, as this paper argues, the Internet can be deceptively problematic. Information can be outdated, statistical data inaccurate, and sources unknown. Learning to critically decipher "information from knowledge" is an essential step in developing well-rounded information literacy. Toward this end, college instructors should encourage students to evaluate Web-based information critically by determining the underlying purpose for a given site, identifying primary source material from secondary summative information, and deciphering the reliability of sources on the basis of an understanding of academic credibility and merit.

Clark, J. H., and Biddle, A. W. *Teaching Critical Thinking: Reports from Across the Curriculum.* New York: Prentice Hall, 1993.

In this collection of essays, the authors introduce a model of critical thinking based on Kolb's learning cycle. They then show how various writing assignments can be used to guide students through the four components of the learning cycle: data gathering, theory building, theory testing, and data-generating processes. Writing assignments that require students to link factual information with interpretive skills serve to enhance students' data-gathering skills. Writing that forces students to weigh alternative perspectives for the purpose of developing a defensible theory reinforces their theory-building capacity. Writing assignments intended to help students sort out implications for the ideas they create strengthens their theory-testing capability. Finally, writing as a vehicle for resolving problems enhances students' data-generating skills.

Bean, J. C. *Engaging Ideas: The Professor's Guide to Integrating Writing, Critical Thinking, and Active Learning in the Classroom.* San Francisco: Jossey-Bass, 1996.

This book serves as a practical guide for instructors wishing to design provocative writing and critical thinking activities for the college classroom.

It offers examples of how college instructors can encourage inquiry, exploration, discussion, and debate in their courses. Likewise, there are a number of strategies for stimulating active learning, coaching writing and critical thinking, structuring assignments, and offering students constructive criticism.

Marzano, R. J. "What Are the General Skills of Thinking and Reasoning and How Do You Teach Them?" *Clearing House*, 1988, *71*(5), 268–273.
    This paper tackles two important issues: What are the skills of thinking and reasoning, and how should thinking and reasoning be taught? By examining seventeen national standards across twelve key subject areas, Marzano identifies six thinking and reasoning skills most often used in a disciplinary context. He then offers a number of suggestions for how thinking and reasoning should be taught, including creating "authentic" tasks that impel students to resolve subject-specific problems and designing curricula that intentionally address the six general thinking skill areas.

Chaffee, J. *Thinking Critically* (7th ed.). Boston: Houghton Mifflin, 2002.
    This book identifies the basic thinking, reasoning, reading, and writing skills required for academic success in the community college classroom. *Thinking Critically* is designed to introduce teachers and students to the cognitive processes that support higher-order thinking and communication skills. In the seventh edition of this book, Chaffee offers timely and valuable exercises, discussion topics, and writing assignments designed to encourage students to interrogate their beliefs and ways of viewing the world.

Moek, W. M. "R(e)Defining the Liberal Arts: Critical Thinking at the Community College Level." Paper presented at the Community College Humanities Association, Eastern Division Conference, New York, Oct. 2002. (ED 471 541)
    It is argued that community college instructors within the humanities are perfectly positioned to have a significant impact upon students' development of critical thinking skills. Unlike at four-year colleges and universities, the community college's historical preparatory function predisposes students toward seeking out individual developmental goals, including their capacity to think critically. Using evidence from his own experiences in the classroom, the author proposes useful strategies for engaging students in free-form discussion designed to enhance student-to-student interaction, as well as individual student critique of course reading assignments and general course content.

Arburn, T., and Bethell, L. J. "Assisting At-Risk Community College Students: Acquisition of Critical Learning Strategies." Paper presented at the annual meeting of the National Association for Research in Science Teaching, Boston, Mar. 1999. (ED 448 016)

Given that a large percentage of community college students fall into the category of at-risk or are first-generation college attendees, it is critical that community colleges develop meaningful, relevant course content that engages them in their learning. This quasi-experimental study focused upon two groups of community college students enrolled in a preprofessional allied health program. The experimental group participated in a combined lecture and student-generated questioning classroom design, while the control group was given a basic lecture format. Findings from this study did not demonstrate a marked difference in overall academic performance between the two groups, but there was improvement in the experimental group's ability to use inferential and deductive skills in course assignments.

Kloss, R. J. "A Nudge is Best: Helping Students Through the Perry Scheme of Intellectual Development." *Journal of College Teaching,* 1994, 42(4), 151–158.
  The Perry scheme of intellectual development is one of the few student development schemes with practical classroom application. Drawing upon his ten years of experience incorporating these strategies into the classroom, Kloss describes the progressive stages of critical thinking observed among his students and offers concrete suggestions on how to challenge students to develop beyond the initial dualist stage to a relativistic world view.

Williams, R. L., and Worth, S. L. "Thinking Skills and Work Habits: Contributors to Course Performance." *Journal of General Education,* 2003, 51(3), 200–227.
  This study attempts to identify the critical thinking skills and work habits that best predict positive student outcomes. Based on a quantitative assessment of the working and thinking habits of 292 undergraduates, Williams and Worth found that critical thinking, classroom attendance, and the quality of individual note taking served as notable predictors in student performance measures within general education courses.

The Foundation for Critical Thinking (http://www.criticalthinking.org)
  The Foundation for Critical Thinking currently houses the Center for Critical Thinking, the National Council for Excellence in Critical Thinking, and the International Center for the Assessment of Higher Order Learning. Information on all three organizations can be found on the foundation's Web site. The Center for Critical Thinking is charged with conducting and disseminating advanced research on critical thinking, and several books and other publications are available on the site:

Nosich, G. *Learning to Think Things Through: A Guide to Critical Thinking Across the Curriculum* (2nd ed.). Upper Saddle River, N.J.: Prentice Hall, 2005.

Paul, R., and Elder, L. *The Thinkers Guide Series*. Dillon Beach, Calif.: Foundation for Critical Thinking. http://www.criticalthinking.org/resources/tgs/. Accessed Feb. 9, 2005.
Paul, R., and Elder, L. *Critical Thinking: Tools for Taking Charge of Your Learning and Your Life*. Upper Saddle River, N.J.: Prentice Hall, 2001.
Nosich, G. *Reasons and Arguments*. Belmont, Calif.: Wadsworth, 1982.
    In addition to these and other publications, the foundation's Web site also offers an array of useful resources for postsecondary educators, including basic definitional and philosophical discussions on critical thinking.

## Tools for Assessing Critical Thinking Skills

As Chapter Two of this volume demonstrates, assessment is essential in developing a comprehensive critical thinking program on a community college campus. As such, assessment of students' critical thinking skills should be conducted thoughtfully and strategically. With a multitude of assessment instruments currently on the market, it is essential that an institution select testing tools that evaluate the skills most relevant to its institutional and classroom contexts and that offer the most accurate measure of students' relative growth and development. As a compliment to the tools presented in Chapter Two, here is a useful compilation of resources designed to assist community college faculty and administrators in determining the appropriate assessment tools for their campus.

Facione, P. A. "Critical Thinking: A Statement of Expert Consensus for Purposes of Educational Assessment and Instruction." Millbrae: California Academic Press, 1990. http://www.insightassessment.com/pdf_files/DEXadobe.PDF. Accessed March 31, 2005.
    Known as the "Delphi Report," this publication defines critical thinking as a process by which individuals form judgments about what to believe or do in a given context. Moreover, it argues that to be critical a person draws from a core set of cognitive skills—analysis, interpretation, inference, explanation, evaluation, and self-regulation—both to form an initial judgment and to monitor and improve the quality of that judgment. These six skills were determined to be essential to developing expert practice and functioning. This report offers helpful suggestions for instructional and assessment practices.

U.S. Department of Education. "The NPEC Sourcebook on Assessment. Vol. I: Definitions and Assessment Methods for Critical Thinking, Problem Solving, and Writing." Washington, D.C.: U.S. Department of Education. http://nces.ed.gov/pubsearch/pubsinfo.asp?pubid=2000195. Accessed Feb. 9, 2005.
    In 1994, Congress authorized the National Postsecondary Education Cooperative (NPEC) to promote information and data at the federal, state,

and institutional levels on postsecondary student learning outcomes. NPEC's sourcebook serves as a valuable compendium of relevant information on assessment testing for postsecondary institutions interested in measuring student outcomes in the areas of critical thinking, problem solving, and writing. This report includes a detailed explanation of conceptual and methodological considerations for deciding on appropriate assessment instruments to use on college campuses.

U.S. Department of Education. "Defining and Assessing Learning: Exploring Competency-Based Initiatives. Report of the National Postsecondary Education Cooperative Working Group on Competency-Based Initiatives in Postsecondary Education." Washington, D.C.: U.S. Department of Education. http://nces.ed.gov/pubs2002/2002159.pdf. Accessed Feb. 9, 2005.

This document examines use of competency-based initiatives among postsecondary institutions in the United States and presents principles, drawn from selected case studies, that underlie successful implementation. Supported by the National Postsecondary Education Cooperative, this project was informed by a working group of experts focusing on how to best use various competencies in a number of educational and work settings. Of particular relevance is the use of critical thinking in completing competency-based tasks within a variety of academic settings.

California Academic Press and Insight Assessment (http://www.insight assessment.com)

The California Academic Press and Insight Assessment offer a range of assessment tools designed to measure students' critical thinking skills. In addition to the California Critical Thinking Skills Test (CCTST), described in detail in Chapter Two, Insight Assessment offers the Test of Everyday Reasoning (TER), the California Reasoning Appraisal (CRA), the Quant-Q, and a dispositional instrument entitled the California Measure of Mental Motivation (CM3). The skills-based tests are designed to measure inductive and deductive reasoning, inference, and analysis, while the dispositional instrument focuses on individual motivational attributes for using reasoning skills. Finally, Insight Assessment has also developed the popular Holistic Critical Thinking Scoring Rubric (HCTSR), which can be administered to college faculty and students alike to measure conceptual understandings of critical thinking, intellectual habits, and individual traits and dispositions.

## Critical Thinking from an Organizational Perspective

How institutions support development of critical thinking skills among students is an important step toward developing a critical thinking culture on campus. Institutions that are able to promote reflection, model quality judgment, and develop a systemic approach to critical engagement will inevitably foster student intellectual development. These resources are designed to assist community college campuses in creating an effective critical thinking culture.

Tsui, L. "Effects of Campus Culture on Students' Critical Thinking." *Review of Higher Education,* 2000, 23(4), 421–441.

A significant amount of research has been conducted on the academic factors contributing to development of students' critical thinking skills; far less focus has been given to the out-of-classroom experiences that may enhance students' intellectual development. This article elaborates on the expanding body of research focused on how organizational culture can enhance development of critical thinking skill. Highlighting qualitative data gleaned from four separate institutional case studies, findings point to the impact of an institution's epistemological orientation in shaping student values toward learning. The study also found that greater emphasis should be given to organizational congruence between classroom instructional priorities, such as critical thinking development, and the institutional reward structures that support teaching. Finally, institutions of higher learning can better facilitate critical thinking by encouraging students to use these tacit skills in all aspects of their collegiate experience.

Robinson, S. "Teaching Critical Thinking at the Community College." Unpublished manuscript, Valencia Community College, 1996. (ED 433 877)

This document reports on efforts at Valencia Community College (Florida) to incorporate critical thinking into its stated core competencies, and to establish critical thinking as a foundational skill among its graduates. The college's *Competency One* states that graduates should be prepared to "think critically and make reasoned choices by acquiring, analyzing, synthesizing, and evaluating knowledge" (p. 2). Valencia Community College also identifies a host of subcompetencies that can serve as replicable models for institutional programming at other campuses.

Neal, E., and Richlin, L. (eds.). *To Improve the Academy: Resources for Faculty, Instructional, and Organizational Development, Vol. 22.* Bolton, Mass.: Anker, 2004.

This annual publication contains seventeen papers on strategies for assessing and evaluating institutional practices in the area of faculty development, instruction, and institutional transformation. Although the journal focuses primarily on four-year college and university practices, section twenty-one, titled "Improving Students' Critical Thinking Outcomes: A Process-Learning Strategy in Eight Steps," introduces an eight-step strategy for improving student development outcomes through curricular enhancement across the disciplines.

## Conclusion

In addition to what is presented in this chapter, there exists a wealth of resource material on the topic of critical thinking. For instance, a multitude of studies target the relationship of specific thinking skills or work habits to academic performance and other developmental outcomes (see, for example, Lawson, 1999; McCutcheon, Hanson, Apperson, and Wynn, 1992; Smith, 1977; Terenzini, Springer, Pascarella, and Nora, 1995; Williams and Eggert, 2002). Similarly, there are disparate views about to how to standardize and assess students' critical thinking skills (see, for example, Ennis, Millman, and Tomko, 1985; Facione, 1986; Facione and Facione, 1994; Halpern, 1988, 1993, 2000; Jones, 1995). The large-scale attention given to these issues reflects the importance of critical thinking as a cognitive and motivational trait that is in congruence with two-year college vocational and educational goals.

Community college faculty, staff, and administrators are perfectly positioned to serve as the primary deliverers of critical thinking skills to our nation's postsecondary students. By building upon a substantive understanding of critical thinking, thoughtful strategies for engaging students, insistence upon questioning the problems found within conventional disciplinary content, and an ability to transform institutional culture to support intellectual development, community colleges markedly expand their capability for preparing students to succeed within the complex and challenging modern-day workplace.

## References

Bower, B. H., and Hardy, K. P. *From Distance Education to E-Learning: Lessons Along the Way.* New Directions for Community Colleges, no. 128. San Francisco: Jossey-Bass, 2004.

Ennis, R. H., Millman, J., and Tomko, T. N. *Cornell Critical Thinking Tests Level X and Level Z* (3rd ed.). Pacific Grove, Calif.: Midwest, 1985.

Facione, P. A. "Testing College-Level Critical Thinking." *Liberal Education,* 1986, 72(3), 221–231.

Facione, P. A. "Critical Thinking: A Statement of Expert Consensus for Purposes of Educational Assessment and Instruction." Millbrae: California Academic Press, 1990. http://www.insightassessment.com/pdf_files/DEXadobe.PDF. Accessed March 31, 2005.

Facione, P. A., and Facione, N. C. *The California Critical Thinking Skills Test: Test Manual.* Millbrae: California Academic Press, 1994.

Halpern, D. F. "Assessing Student Outcomes for Psychology Majors." *Teaching of Psychology,* 1988, 15(4), 181–186.

Halpern, D. F. "Assessing the Effectiveness of Critical Thinking Instruction." *Journal of General Education,* 1993, 42(4), 239–254.

Halpern, D. F. "Teaching for Critical Thinking: Helping College Students Develop the Skills and Dispositions for a Critical Thinker." In M. D. Svinicki (ed.), *Teaching and Learning on the Edge of the Millennium: Building on What We Have Learned.* New Directions for Teaching and Learning, no. 80. San Francisco: Jossey-Bass, 2000.

Hirose, S. "Critical Thinking in Community Colleges. ERIC Digest." Los Angeles: ERIC Clearinghouse for Community Colleges, University of California, Los Angeles, 1992. http://www.ericdigests.org/1992–2/critical.htm. Accessed Jan. 20, 2005.

Jones, E. A. *The National Assessment of College Student Learning: Identifying College Graduates, Essential Skills in Writing, Speech, and Listening, and Critical Thinking.* Washington, D.C.: National Center for Educational Statistics, U.S. Department of Education, 1995.

Lawson, T. J. "Assessing Psychological Critical Thinking as a Learning Outcome for Psychology Majors." *Teaching of Psychology,* 1999, *26(3),* 207–208.

McCutcheon, L. E., Hanson, E., Apperson, J., and Wynn, V. "Relationships Among Critical Thinking Skills, Academic Achievement, and Misconceptions." *Psychological Reports,* 1992, *71,* 635–639.

Smith, D. "College Classroom Interactions and Critical Thinking." *Journal of Educational Psychology,* 1977, *69(2),* 180–190.

Terenzini, P. T., Springer, L., Pascarella, E. T., and Nora, A. "Influences Affecting the Development of Students' Critical Thinking Skills." *Research in Higher Education,* 1995, *36(1),* 23–29.

Tsui, L. "Effects of Campus Culture on Students' Critical Thinking." *Review of Higher Education,* 2000, *23(4),* 421–441.

Williams, R. L., and Eggert, A. C. "Notetaking in College Classes: Student Patterns and Instructional Strategies." *Journal of General Education,* 2002, *51(3),* 173–194.

*SHANNON M. CALDERONE is a doctoral student in Higher Education and Organizational Change at the University of California, Los Angeles.*

# INDEX

# Back Issue/Subscription Order Form

Copy or detach and send to:
**Jossey-Bass, A Wiley Imprint, 989 Market Street, San Francisco CA 94103-1741**

**Call or fax toll-free: Phone 888-378-2537 6:30AM – 3PM PST; Fax 888-481-2665**

Back Issues:      Please send me the following issues at $29 each
(Important: please include ISBN number with your order.)

_____

_____

_____

$ _____     Total for single issues

$ _____     SHIPPING CHARGES: SURFACE    Domestic Canadian

|  | First Item | $5.00 | $6.00 |
|---|---|---|---|
|  | Each Add'l Item | $3.00 | $1.50 |

For next-day and second-day delivery rates, call the number listed above.

Subscriptions     Please __ start __ renew my subscription to *New Directions for Community Colleges* for the year 2____ at the following rate:

| U.S. | __ Individual $80 | __ Institutional $170 |
|---|---|---|
| Canada | __ Individual $80 | __ Institutional $210 |
| All Others | __ Individual $104 | __ Institutional $244 |

Online subscriptions are available too!

**For more information about online subscriptions visit
www.interscience.wiley.com**

$ _____     Total single issues and subscriptions (Add appropriate sales tax for your state for single issue orders. No sales tax for U.S. subscriptions. Canadian residents, add GST for subscriptions and single issues.)

__Payment enclosed (U.S. check or money order only)
__VISA __ MC __ AmEx __ # _____ Exp. Date _____

Signature _____ Day Phone _____
__ Bill Me (U.S. institutional orders only. Purchase order required.)

Purchase order # _____
     **Federal Tax ID13559302**         **GST 89102 8052**

Name _____

Address _____

_____

Phone _____ E-mail _____

For more information about Jossey-Bass, visit our Web site at www.josseybass.com

CC125   Legal Issues in the Community College
        *Robert C. Cloud*
        Community colleges must be prepared for lawsuits, federal statutes, court
        rulings, union negotiations, and other legal issues that could affect
        institutional stability and effectiveness. This volume provides leaders with
        information about board relations, tenure and employment, student rights
        and safety, disability law, risk management, copyright and technology
        issues, and more.
        ISBN:    0-7879-7482-X

CC124   Successful Approaches to Fundraising and Development
        *Mark David Milliron, Gerardo E. de los Santos, Boo Browning*
        This volume outlines how community colleges can tap into financial support
        from the private sector, as four-year institutions have been doing. Chapter
        authors discuss building community college foundations, cultivating
        relationships with the local community, generating new sources of revenue,
        fundraising from alumni, and the roles of boards, presidents, and trustees.
        ISBN:    0-7879-7283-5

CC123   Help Wanted: Preparing Community College Leaders in a New Century
        *William E. Piland, David B. Wolf*
        This issue brings together various thoughtful perspectives on the nature of
        leading community colleges over the foreseeable future. Authors offer
        suggestions for specific programmatic actions that community colleges
        themselves can take to provide the quantity, quality, specializations, and
        diversity of leaders that are needed.
        ISBN:    0-7879-7248-7

CC122   Classification Systems for Two-Year Colleges
        *Alexander C. McCormick, Rebecca D. Cox*
        This critically important volume advances the conversation among
        researchers and practitioners about possible approaches to classifying two-
        year colleges. After an introduction to the history, purpose, practice, and
        pitfalls of classifying colleges and universities, five different classification
        schemes are presented, followed by commentary by knowledgable
        respondents representing potential users of a classification system:
        community college associations, institutional leaders, and researchers. The
        final chapter applies the five proposed schemes to a sample of colleges for
        purposes of illustration.
        ISBN:    0-7879-7171-5

CC121   The Role of the Community College in Teacher Education
        *Barbara K. Townsend, Jan M. Ignash*
        Illustrates the extent to which community colleges have become major
        players in teacher education, not only in the traditional way of providing the
        first two years of an undergraduate degree in teacher education but in more
        controversial ways such as offering associate and baccalaureate degrees in
        teacher education and providing alternative certification programs.
        ISBN:    0-7879-6868-4

CC120   Enhancing Community Colleges Through Professional Development
        *Gordon E. Watts*
        Offers a much needed perspective on the expanding role of professional
        development in community colleges. Chapter authors provide descriptions
        of how their institutions have addressed issues through professional

development, created institutional change, developed new delivery systems for professional development, reached beyond development just for faculty, and found new uses for traditional development activities.
ISBN:    0-7879-6330-5

CC119    **Developing Successful Partnerships with Business and the Community**
*Mary S. Spangler*
Demonstrates that there are many different approaches to community colleges' partnering with the private sector and that when partners are actively engaged in tailoring education, training, and learning to their students, everyone is the beneficiary.
ISBN:    0-7879-6321-9

CC118    **Community College Faculty: Characteristics, Practices, and Challenges**
*Charles Outcalt*
Offers multiple perspectives on the ways community college faculty fulfill their complex professional roles. With data from national surveys, this volume provides an overview of community college faculty, looks at their primary teaching responsibility, and examines particular groups of instructors, including part-timers, women, and people of color.
ISBN:    0-7879-6328-3

CC117    **Next Steps for the Community College**
*Trudy H. Bers, Harriott D. Calhoun*
Provides an overview of relevant literature and practice covering major community college topics: transfer rates, vocational education, remedial and developmental education, English as a second language education, assessment of student learning, student services, faculty and staff, and governance and policy. Includes a chapter discussing the categories, types, and purposes of literature about community colleges and the major publications germane to community college practitioners and scholars.
ISBN:    0-7879-6289-9

CC116    **The Community College Role in Welfare to Work**
*C. David Lisman*
Provides examples of effective programs including a job placement program meeting the needs of rural welfare recipients, short-term and advanced levels of technical training, a call center program for customer service job training, beneficial postsecondary training, collaborative programs for long-term family economic self-sufficiency, and a family-based approach recognizing the needs of welfare recipients and their families.
ISBN:    0-7879-5781-X

CC115    **The New Vocationalism in Community Colleges**
*Debra D. Bragg*
Analyzes the role of community college leaders in developing programs, successful partnerships and collaboration with communities, work-based learning, changes in perception of terminal education and transfer education, changing instructional practices for changing student populations and the integration of vocational education into the broader agenda of American higher education.
ISBN:    0-7879-5780-1

CC114    Transfer Students: Trends and Issues
*Frankie Santos Laanan*
Evaluates recent research and policy discussions surrounding transfer students, and summarizes three broad themes in transfer policy: research, student and academic issues, and institutional factors. Argues that institutions are in a strategic position to provide students with programs for rigorous academic training as well as opportunities to participate in formal articulation agreements with senior institutions.
ISBN:    0-7879-5779-8

CC113    Systems for Offering Concurrent Enrollment at High Schools and Community Colleges
*Piedad F. Robertson, Brian G. Chapman, Fred Gaskin*
Offers approaches to creating valuable programs, detailing all the components necessary for the success and credibility of concurrent enrollment. Focuses on the faculty liaisons from appropriate disciplines that provide the framework for an ever-improving program.
ISBN:    0-7879-5758-5

CC112    Beyond Access: Methods and Models for Increasing Retention and Learning Among Minority Students
*Steven R. Aragon*
Presents practical models, alternative approaches and new strategies for creating effective cross-cultural courses that foster higher retention and learning success for minority students. Argues that educational programs must now develop a broader curriculum that includes multicultural and multi-linguistic information.
ISBN:    0-7879-5429-2

CC111    How Community Colleges Can Create Productive Collaborations with Local Schools
*James C. Palmer*
Details ways that community colleges and high schools can work together to help students navigate the difficult passage from secondary to higher education. Provides detailed case studies of actual collaborations between specific community colleges and high school districts, discuss legal problems that can arise when high school students enroll in community colleges, and more.
ISBN:    0-7879-5428-4

CC110    Building Successful Relationships Between Community Colleges and the Media
*Clifton Truman Daniel, Hanel Henriksen Hastings*
Explores current relationships between two-year colleges and the media across the country, reviewing the history of community colleges' relationships with members of the press, examining the media's relationships with community college practitioners, and offering practical strategies for advancing an institution's visibility.
ISBN:    0-7879-5427-6

# NEW DIRECTIONS FOR COMMUNITY COLLEGES IS NOW AVAILABLE ONLINE AT WILEY INTERSCIENCE

## What is Wiley InterScience?

*Wiley InterScience* is the dynamic online content service from John Wiley & Sons delivering the full text of over 300 leading scientific, technical, medical, and professional journals, plus major reference works, the acclaimed *Current Protocols* laboratory manuals, and even the full text of select Wiley print books online.

## What are some special features of Wiley InterScience?

*Wiley InterScience Alerts* is a service that delivers table of contents via e-mail for any journal available on Wiley InterScience as soon as a new issue is published online.
*Early View* is Wiley's exclusive service presenting individual articles online as soon as they are ready, even before the release of the compiled print issue. These articles are complete, peer-reviewed, and citable.
*CrossRef* is the innovative multi-publisher reference linking system enabling readers to move seamlessly from a reference in a journal article to the cited publication, typically located on a different server and published by a different publisher.

## How can I access Wiley InterScience?

Visit http://www.interscience.wiley.com

*Guest Users* can browse Wiley InterScience for unrestricted access to journal Tables of Contents and Article Abstracts, or use the powerful search engine.
*Registered Users* are provided with a *Personal Home Page* to store and manage customized alerts, searches, and links to favorite journals and articles. Additionally, Registered Users can view free Online Sample Issues and preview selected material from major reference works.
*Licensed Customers* are entitled to access full-text journal articles in PDF, with select journals also offering full-text HTML.

## How do I become an Authorized User?

*Authorized Users* are individuals authorized by a paying Customer to have access to the journals in Wiley InterScience. For example, a university that subscribes to Wiley journals is considered to be the Customer. Faculty, staff and students authorized by the university to have access to those journals in Wiley InterScience are Authorized Users. Users should contact their Library for information on which Wiley journals they have access to in Wiley InterScience.

## ASK YOUR INSTITUTION ABOUT WILEY INTERSCIENCE TODAY!

# As Old As Time

# As Old As Time

## A Culinary Odyssey Using Flavored Olive Oils and Balsamic Vinegars

MICHELE CASTELLANO SENAC

*Michele Castellano Senac*

There Are Diamonds In The Sky

ISBN: 978-0-692-30534-8

First Edition

All photos by Lorrie Castellano unless otherwise noted.

Design by Kay Turnbaugh

Other books by the author

*Around the Table, A Culinary Memoir by Two Sisters*
by Michele Castellano Senac and Lorrie Castellano

Dedicated To Jeremy

Long may you cook.
Long may you surf.

# CONTENTS

# Part Two – Recipes

# INTRODUCTION

Olive oil and I go back a long way. My earliest memories come from times spent with my mother and grandmother in the kitchen, planning and cooking meals, setting the table, and eventually sitting down to eat a delicious, satisfying meal. Those experiences have carried me into adulthood and are an important part of my life today. Some of my happiest times have been sitting around the table enjoying a great meal with family and friends.

My mother and grandmother used olive oil for everything. I never remember my mother measuring anything, including olive oil. She would take the large gold and black decorated gallon tin of olive oil that was stored in a kitchen cabinet and splash it into all her recipes. Somehow, she knew just the right amount to use.

No matter the state of the family budget, my mother purchased the best olive oil she could afford because she knew how important it was to the meals she prepared. She advised me to do the same. She knew what she was talking about when she said to buy the freshest olive oil available. Using high quality olive oil makes all the difference in the flavor, appearance and health benefits of foods. Thankfully, today high quality, fresh Extra-Virgin Olive Oil is easily available, along with considerable information about the health benefits.

My grandmother believed in the miracle properties of olive oil. Many warm spring and summer days she would call my cousin and me outside to sit on folding chairs in the sun while she massaged olive oil onto our faces and into our scalps. When we protested that the olive oil was running into our eyes, she waved away our complaints saying, "One day you'll be glad I did this because it will keep your skin and hair healthy." Many personal hair and skin products now tout the same promise my grandmother made years ago.

Growing up, red wine vinegar was an everyday part of a meal. My mother served it on a leafy green salad and on many fresh vegetables each night at supper. The wine vinegar she used was homemade. The red wine came from a family member or friend who made wine in their basement, as was the custom in many Italian-American homes. My mother always had an uncorked bottle of red wine in a kitchen cabinet, and she kept it there until it turned into vinegar. Years later, I was introduced to balsamic vinegar and loved it and use it today. Red wine vinegar is still enjoyable and is reminiscent of my mother using it in a salad or drizzling it on vegetables.

From those early memories and experiences, I gained a love of good food and good ingredients and their importance in our everyday lives. It's no wonder that I was drawn to an amazing specialty shop, Palmetto Olive Oil Company, in Greenville, South Carolina, where I live. It was there, first as a customer, and then as an employee, that my culinary world expanded. I was introduced to a tasty variety of flavored olive oils and balsamic vinegars, as well as Ultra-Premium Extra-Virgin Olive Oils. Working at the shop, I come in contact with hundreds of customers each year. I listened and learned what they wanted: a simple, informative book on how to use these products to their full potential, how to incorporate them into a healthy diet, and how to prepare delicious, nutritious meals for themselves, their families and friends.

This book is intended to give the reader an introduction to many of the Ultra-Premium Extra-Virgin Olive Oils, flavored Olive Oils, and Dark and White Balsamic Vinegars available — a beginning of a culinary odyssey. As you turn the pages, join with me in discovering these foods that are as old as time and as mysterious and mystical as life itself.

Michele Castellano Senac

# PART ONE

# Mysteries and Myths of Olive Oil

Olive oil and balsamic vinegar, now commonplace staples in most kitchen pantries, are ancient foods surrounded in mystery, mysticism and magic. Noted in numerous ancient texts, including the Bible and the Torah, the olive has held a special place in the history of humankind for thousands of years.

Harvesting methods of olives have been depicted on pottery dating to 500 B.C. Wall paintings depict olive trees growing in ancient Egypt. Olive branches were found in the tomb of King Tut. Olive oil was a staple in ancient diets around the world, and its use spread along trade routes into Italy, France, Spain and the African coast.

Today olive trees are grown in many parts of the world, from the Middle East to South America, and olive oil is exported around the globe.

Greek mythology depicts Athena, Goddess of Wisdom, giving an olive tree to the Greeks as a gift. It was planted on the top of the Acropolis and from there offshoots were planted throughout the region. Olive oil was a part of everyday life, used in ceremonies, celebrations, religious events, and as a medicine. Olive oil was used to anoint people, from the ordinary citizen to the monarchs. People wore wreaths of olive branches on their heads for decoration as well as to symbolize peace and to invite abundance into their lives. Additionally, the olive has long been the symbol of goodness, nobility, perseverance and permanence.

# Secrets and Superstitions of Balsamic Vinegar

Up until a few years ago, true balsamic vinegar was hardly available in the United States. Although balsamic vinegar has been made for nearly a thousand years in Modena and Reggio in Italy, it was known only to a select group of wealthy families who kept it as a guarded, prized secret. Its origin is ancient, and it was made in small batches and handed down from generation to generation. Flasks with traces of balsamic vinegar have been found in Egyptian tombs which may be indicative of how much it was revered. Its first historical reference was in 1046 A.D. when a bottle of balsamic vinegar was given by royalty as a gift to an honored friend.

## Warding Off Evil Spirits

Balsamic vinegar has been known through the ages not only for its flavor, but for its health benefit. During the Middle Ages it was produced specifically for medicinal value. Sipped as a remedy to the plague, as an appetite stimulant, and as a treatment for everything from sore throat to heart problems, it was highly valued for its curative properties. Some believed that it could ward off evil spirits and deflect negative energies. Others believed balsamic vinegar was a symbol of friendship and love. Because it takes so many years to transform into the tasty condiment that it is, the making of balsamic vinegar is surrounded in mystery, and each family's recipe is shrouded in secrecy.

Today, good quality balsamic vinegar is readily available and is showing up in many American kitchens. Using it in salads, marinades, deserts and cooking, we have discovered what the ancients have known for centuries — that a few drops can transform any dish into a tasty delight.

## The Making of Balsamic Vinegar

Balsamic vinegar is made from boiled down fresh grape juice, called grape must, and aged in a series of progressively smaller barrels made of different woods, where it spends a minimum of 12 years to decades, until it becomes a sweet, syrupy, rich condiment. True balsamic vinegar is known in Italy as "aceto balsamic tradizionale."

## Things You Should Know About Olive Oil Before Purchasing

HARVEST ⟳ To ensure freshness, it's helpful to know where the olives are grown and the date they are pressed. Olives grown in the northern hemisphere usually are harvested and pressed between September and January. Olives grown in the southern hemisphere usually are harvested and pressed from May to July. For optimum flavor, olive oil should be on the shelf for sale within a few months after press date.

THE PRESS  For maximum freshness and flavor, olives should be rushed quickly to the press after harvesting. Delay causes fermentation to occur which spoils the flavor. The process for pressing olives is extensive and there is detailed information available for further study. Cold pressings, where no heat or chemicals are used in the process, and first pressings, where no water or solvents are applied to the pressed paste, are best.

GRADES  There are many grades of olive oil and there are many ways that olive oil can be altered that affects flavor and quality. The International Olive Oil Council (IOOC) states that Extra-Virgin Olive Oil must meet four criteria: it must be made from the mechanical extraction of olives, be cold-pressed, have an acidity level of less than 1%, and have a perfect taste. Ultra Premium (UP) is a new category of olive oil that distinguishes the highest quality of olive oil in the world. The UP standard was created by Veronica Foods in Oakland, California, in response to the growing need to separate high quality Extra-Virgin Olive Oils from what dominates the so-called "gourmet" and "premium" olive oil markets. In order to qualify for the UP grade, Extra-Virgin Olive Oil must meet or exceed a comprehensive set of production, storage, transportation, testing, chemistry and organoleptic (involving the use of the sense organs) requirements.

TASTE  Olive oil taste is affected by climate, soil, the care in how the olives are grown, handled and pressed. Pure olive oil can be mild, medium, or robust in taste. This is due to the polyphenol (antioxidant) count, which contains the health benefits of olive oil. The higher the polyphenol count, the more intense or robust the oil is. It's important to taste the oil before purchasing. That is why purchasing from a specialty shop, where tasting is available and encouraged, is best.

FRYING  Frying with olive oil seals in moisture and creates a crispy crust. Some information says that heat will eliminate the fruity flavor of Extra-Virgin Olive Oil. Virgin olive oils remain stable at fairly high temperatures because of a low polyphenol count. Other information suggests that using quality Extra-Virgin Olive Oil is best because it has a low smoke point, whereas lower quality oil has a lower smoke point. There seems to be some agreement that the preferred high temperature for olive oil in order to retain its highest benefit is somewhere between 365°F and 400°F. I use fresh, high quality Extra-Virgin Olive Oil in all my cooking, including sautéing and frying, and find that it retains its good flavor no matter the temperature.

## Things You Should Know About Balsamic Vinegar Before Purchasing

QUALITY ∿ True balsamic vinegar, or aceto balsamic tradizionale, was relatively unknown in the United States until the 1970s. As chefs began using it and travelers to Italy discovered it, awareness and use began to grow. Producers could not keep up with the demand and short-cuts were taken and inferior balsamic vinegars began to appear on the market. In 1987, in order to maintain quality, the provinces of Modena and Reggio in Italy were granted dual Domain of Control (DOC). Only vinegars that meet their requirements can be called aceto balsamic trandizionale. Since 1998, the Consortium of Balsamic Vinegar of Modena has issued a product certification, Protected Geographic Indication (PGI), which assures consumers that the balsamic vinegar is from the authenticated area.

PRICE ∿ Balsamic vinegar can be purchased for as little as $4 for a 750-milliliter bottle, or as much as $535 for a 3-ounce bottle. Aging is a criterion for fine balsamic vinegar, though that may be misleading because vinegar that touts being aged 10 years, may have a small amount of older vinegar added to it. Volumes have been written about the price and quality of balsamic vinegar. Simply put, buy the best you can afford that has the taste that pleases you.

TASTE ∿ There is a lot of controversy about what determines good balsamic vinegar. Ultimately it is taste that determines the quality of the vinegar. Balsamic vinegars range in characteristics from sweet, to thick, to woody. Others are bitter or overly acidic. Be sure to taste the vinegar before purchasing. Buy from a specialty shop according to your palate and pocketbook.

TYPES ∞ There are three levels of artisan-style aceto balsamico tradizionale vinegars: tradizionale, qualita superior, and the highest extra vecchio. These are foiled, stamped and costly. A relatively recent category is made by small producers who follow traditional artisan methods, but who are not members of the Consortium Producers due to cost, but could qualify for the tradizionale category. These are called condimenti and differ from the industrially produced blended vinegars that go by that name. These vinegars can still be expensive, but many are priced within reason.

# Quick Guide to Using Olive Oils & Balsamic Vinegars

There is much more information in the individual oils and vinegars section of this book, but here is a quick guide.

## ∽ OLIVE OILS ∾

### In Cooking:

» Salad dressing either alone or paired with a balsamic vinegar

» Dipping bread

» As a marinade either alone or paired with a balsamic vinegar

» Drizzle over potatoes, rice, quinoa, couscous, tabouli, vegetables, meat, fish, and poultry before grilling or roasting

» Sautéing vegetables

» Add to stew, soups, or to toss pasta

» Use in place of butter, margarine, vegetable or canola oil, including for baking

» Drizzle over bread, salt and/or herbs and toast in oven or broiler

» Place in an oil mister, using it instead of aerosol spray oils

» Anytime you want your food to taste like a gourmet chef prepared it

### For Personal Use:

» Moisturizer and conditioner for skin, nails, cuticles, hair and scalp

» Eye make-up remover

» Polish wood or shine stainless steel

» Remove tar or paint from the skin

## ∽ BALSAMIC VINEGARS ∾

» Salad Dressing either alone or paired with Extra-Virgin Olive Oil

» As a marinade either alone or paired with Extra-Virgin Olive Oil

» Drizzle over fruit, berries, ice cream, cakes, and pastries

» Drizzle over cheese

» As a substitute for sugar to sweeten sauces

» Add to water or sparkling water for flavor

» As a dipping sauce for meats

# Quick Guide to the Health Benefits of Olive Oils & Balsamic Vinegars

## ∾ OLIVE OILS ∾

* Heart healthy by preventing formation of LDL Cholesterol, which is the bad cholesterol
* Helps control blood pressure, reducing the risks of stroke and heart attack
* Inhibits growth of some cancers because of its high anti-oxidant properties
* Helps control blood sugar and triglycerides
* Reduces severity of arthritis, asthma, psoriasis and eczema because of its natural anti-inflammatory properties
* Benefits the stomach by lowering hydrochloric acid levels
* Benefits hair and scalp by hydrating hair follicles, resulting in reduced hair loss and dandruff

## ∾ BALSAMIC VINEGARS ∾

* Decreases risk of heart attack by helping to normalize blood pressure and stabilize cholesterol levels
* Helps with weight stabilization and diabetes control due to its low gylcemic scale, low calorie, sugar, and carbohydrate content
* Helps fight cancer due to its bioflavonoid and anti-oxidant content
* Helps digestive process by stimulating the pepsin enzyme which helps with the absorption of amino acids
* Supports bone health because it contains acetic acid and pepsin which help in the absorption of calcium and magnesium necessary for healthy bones
* Helps with pain relief due to its anti-viral and anti-microbial properties

# USING OLIVE OIL
## &
# BALSAMIC VINEGARS

## TOGETHER
## ᴗAS A PAIRᴗ

*The following is a list of suggested olive oils and vinegars to use together.*

| OIL | INTENSITY* |
|---|---|
| Arbequina | mild/medium |
| Barnea | robust |
| Cerasuola | medium |
| Chemlali | medium |
| Cobrancosa | medium |
| Coratina | robust |
| Empeltre | robust |
| Hojiblanca | mild, medium and robust |
| Koroneiki | medium and robust |
| Leccino | mild, medium and robust |
| Manzanillo | robust |
| Mission | robust |
| Nocellara | mild |
| Oro Bailen Picual | robust |
| Picual | medium/robust |
| Reserva Especial | robust |

*Intensities may vary.

PURE

ULTRA-PREMIUM

EXTRA-VIRGIN

OLIVE

OIL

PAIRINGS

Any of these oils can be paired with any Traditional Dark Balsamic or Premium White Balsamic Vinegars.

# INFUSED AND FUSED
# EXTRA-VIRGIN OLIVE OIL
# PAIRINGS

## Olive Oil
## Basil

Jalapeño Balsamic
Lemongrass Mint Balsamic
Oregano Balsamic
Cinnamon Pear Balsamic
Pineapple Balsamic
Grapefruit Balsamic
Fig Balsamic
Strawberry Balsamic
Raspberry Balsamic

## Olive Oil
## Butter

Coconut Balsamic
Cranberry Pear Balsamic
Maple Balsamic
Black Cherry Balsamic
Strawberry Balsamic
Cinnamon Pear Balsamic
Tahitian Vanilla Balsamic

## Olive Oil
## Chipotle

Pineapple Balsamic
Sicilian Lemon Balsamic
Jalapeño Balsamic
Coconut Balsamic
Honey Ginger Balsamic
Peach Balsamic
Black Cherry Balsamic
Cinnamon Pear Balsamic
Dark Chocolate Balsamic
Dark Espresso Balsamic
Tangerine Balsamic
Maple Balsamic
Raspberry Balsamic

## Olive Oil
## Cilantro and Roasted Onion

Tahitian Vanilla Balsamic
Honey Ginger Balsamic
Lemongrass Mint Balsamic
Peach Balsamic
Coconut Balsamic
Fig Balsamic
Pomegranate Balsamic
Red Apple Balsamic

## Garlic
*Olive Oil*

Sicilian Lemon Balsamic
Apricot Balsamic
Honey Ginger Balsamic
Grapefruit Balsamic
Pineapple Balsamic
Jalapeño Balsamic
Oregano Balsamic
Pomegranate Balsamic
Fig Balsamic
Blackberry Ginger Balsamic
Champagne Balsamic
Raspberry Balsamic

## Harissa
*Olive Oil*

Honey Ginger Balsamic
Pineapple Balsamic
Jalapeño Balsamic
Strawberry Balsamic

## Herbes de Provence
*Olive Oil*

Herbes de Provence
Cranberry Pear Balsamic
Grapefruit Balsamic
Honey Ginger Balsamic
Peach Balsamic
Sicilian Lemon Balsamic
Lavender Balsamic
Pomegranate Balsamic
Champagne Balsamic
Raspberry Balsamic

## Tarragon
*Olive Oil*

Peach Balsamic
Pineapple Balsamic
Sicilian Lemon Balsamic
Raspberry Balsamic
Champagne Balsamic

## Tuscan Herb
*Olive Oil*

Cranberry Pear Balsamic
Apricot Balsamic
Sicilian Lemon Balsamic
Pineapple Balsamic
Peach Balsamic
Blackberry Ginger Balsamic
Black Cherry Balsamic
Champagne Balsamic
Tahitian Vanilla Balsamic
Fig Balsamic
Dark Espresso Balsamic
Strawberry Balsamic

## Wild Mushroom and Sage
*Olive Oil*

Sicilian Lemon Balsamic
Cinnamon Pear Balsamic
Fig Balsamic
Red Apple Balsamic
Tahitian Vanilla Balsamic

# Whole Fruit Fused Olive Oil

## Blood Orange
Olive Oil

Pineapple Balsamic

Cranberry Pear Balsamic

Coconut Balsamic

Blackberry Ginger Balsamic

Cinnamon Pear Balsamic

Dark Chocolate Balsamic

Dark Espresso Balsamic

Red Apple Balsamic

Fig Balsamic

Tahitian Vanilla Balsamic

Maple Balsamic

Blueberry Balsamic

Raspberry Balsamic

## Eureka Lemon
Olive Oil

Coconut Balsamic

Peach Balsamic

Apricot Balsamic

Oregano Balsamic

Cranberry Pear Balsamic

Blackberry Ginger Balsamic

Black Cherry Balsamic

Pomegranate Balsamic

Raspberry Balsamic

Strawberry Balsamic

Blueberry Balsamic

Tangerine Balsamic

Lavender Balsamic

## Persian Lime
Olive Oil

Apricot Balsamic

Coconut Balsamic

Oregano Balsamic

White Balsamic

Pineapple Balsamic

Tangerine Balsamic

Lavender Balsamic

Lemongrass Mint Balsamic

Blackberry Ginger Balsamic

Cranberry Pear Balsamic

Raspberry Balsamic

Strawberry Balsamic

Black Cherry Balsamic

Pomegranate Balsamic

## Baklouti
Olive Oil

Peach Balsamic

Pineapple Balsamic

Honey Ginger Balsamic

Cinnamon Pear Balsamic

Dark Chocolate Balsamic

Raspberry Balsamic

# Whole Herb Fused Olive Oil

**Olive Oil**

## Wild Rosemary

Cranberry Pear Balsamic

Sicilian Lemon Balsamic

Oregano Balsamic

Peach Balsamic

Pomegranate Balsamic

Strawberry Balsamic

Raspberry Balsamic

Black Cherry Balsamic

Fig Balsamic

# Gourmet Oils

## Roasted Sesame Oil

Blackberry Ginger Balsamic Vinegar

Coconut Balsamic Vinegar

Pineapple Balsamic Vinegar

These gourmet oils are typically used as finishing oils. Finishing oils add texture and flavor to a dish. Use sparingly as a little goes a long way.

## Roasted Walnut Oil

Champagne Balsamic Vinegar

Cinnamon Pear Balsamic Vinegar

Coconut Balsamic Vinegar

Blueberry Balsamic Vinegar

Dark Espresso Balsamic Vinegar

Fig Balsamic Vinegar

Pomegranate Balsamic Vinegar

Red Apple Balsamic Vinegar

## White Truffle Oil

Fig Balsamic Vinegar

Sicilian Lemon Balsamic Vinegar

# ⌁ DESCRIPTIONS OF FLAVORED EXTRA-VIRGIN OLIVE OILS ⌁

## Basil

DESCRIPTION: Fresh, green and herbal. Basil and olive oil are two integral ingredients in Mediterranean cooking.

PERFECT WITH: Salads, vegetables, meat, fish, pasta, bread

VINEGAR PAIRINGS: Jalapeño, Lemongrass Mint, Oregano, Cinnamon Pear, Pineapple, Grapefruit, Fig, Strawberry, Raspberry, Blueberry

## Butter

DESCRIPTION: Use this creamy, golden, vegetarian, dairy-free olive oil as a butter substitute in baking or in anything that calls for melted butter.

PERFECT WITH: As a butter substitute

VINEGAR PAIRINGS: Coconut, Cranberry Pear, Maple, Black Cherry, Strawberry, Cinnamon Pear, Tahitian Vanilla

---

Butter Olive Oil is golden, creamy, and can easily be used in most recipes that call for butter. Since it is non-dairy and vegetarian, using it reduces calories without sacrificing flavor. Drizzle it over vegetables, baked potatoes, grits, rice, popcorn, or any foods requiring butter. It can be substituted in many baking recipes, but not all.

Substitute 100% Extra-Virgin Olive Oil for butter/margarine:

| Butter/Margarine | Olive Oil |
|---|---|
| 1 teaspoon | ¾ teaspoon |
| 1 tablespoon | 2 ¼ teaspoons |
| ¼ cup | 3 tablespoons |
| ⅓ cup | ¼ cup |
| ½ cup | ¼ cup + 2 tablespoons |
| ⅔ cup | ½ cup |
| ¾ cup | ½ cup + 1 tablespoon |
| 1 cup | ¾ cup |

## Chipolte

DESCRIPTION: Chili-infused oil with a smoky flavor

PERFECT WITH: Pork, poultry, beef, pasta, vegetables, salads, bread

VINEGAR PAIRINGS: Pineapple, Sicilian Lemon, Jalapeño, Coconut, Honey Ginger, Peach, Black Cherry, Cinnamon Pear, Dark Chocolate, Dark Espresso, Tangerine, Maple, Raspberry

## Cilantro and Roasted Onion

DESCRIPTION: Blended flavors of roasted, sweet cippolini onions and cilantro

PERFECT WITH: Eggs, salads, chicken, bread

VINEGAR PAIRINGS: Tahitian Vanilla, Honey Ginger, Lemongrass Mint, Peach, Coconut, Fig, Pomegranate, Red Apple

## Garlic

DESCRIPTION: The flavor of pungent, fresh garlic. Garlic and olive oil are often used together in Mediterranean cooking.

PERFECT WITH: Pasta, salad, meat, seafood, bread

VINEGAR PAIRINGS: Apricot, Oregano, Pomegranate, Fig, Blackberry Ginger, Champagne, Raspberry

## Harissa

DESCRIPTION: Chili peppers, caraway, coriander and cumin pounded into a paste and left overnight to develop its flavor, with additional peppers to give it a very hot finish

PERFECT WITH: Chicken, meat, eggs, vegetables, bread, and pasta

VINEGAR PAIRINGS: Honey Ginger, Pineapple, Jalapeño, Strawberry

# Herbes de Provence

DESCRIPTION: Smooth notes of savory, thyme and bay leaf

PERFECT WITH: Seafood, pork, beef, poultry, lamb, rice, potatoes, vegetables

VINEGAR PAIRINGS: Cranberry Pear, Grapefruit, Honey Ginger, Peach, Sicilian Lemon, Lavender, Pomegranate, Champagne, Raspberry

# Tarragon

DESCRIPTION: Captures the aroma and flavor of tarragon

PERFECT WITH: Seafood, chicken, salad, pasta, bread, rice, vegetables

VINEGAR PAIRINGS: Peach, Pineapple, Sicilian Lemon, Raspberry, Champagne

# Tuscan Herb

DESCRIPTION: Blend of herbs, sun-dried tomatoes, and garlic

PERFECT WITH: Fish, poultry, beef, vegetables, bread, pasta, rice, risotto

VINEGAR PAIRINGS: Cranberry Pear, Apricot, Sicilian Lemon, Pineapple, Peach, Blackberry Ginger, Black Cherry, Champagne, Tahitian Vanilla, Fig Balsamic, Dark Espresso, Strawberry

# Wild Mushroom and Sage

DESCRIPTION: Fresh herbaceous sage paired with an array of savory wild mushrooms

PERFECT WITH: Pork, poultry, eggs, rice, vegetables, potatoes

VINEGAR PAIRINGS: Sicilian Lemon, White, Cinnamon Pear, Fig, Red Apple, Tahitian Vanilla

# ❧ WHOLE FRUIT FUSED OLIVE OIL ❧

## Blood Orange

DESCRIPTION: Whole blood oranges and Tunisian ripe olives crushed together at the same time

PERFECT WITH: Seafood, chicken, salad, fruit, bread, desserts, in baking

VINEGAR PAIRINGS: Pineapple, Cranberry Pear, Coconut, Blackberry, Cinnamon Pear, Dark Chocolate, Dark Espresso, Red Apple, Fig, Tahitian Vanilla, Maple, Blueberry, Raspberry

## Eureka Lemon

DESCRIPTION: Whole, fresh lemons and late harvest olives crushed together at the same time

PERFECT WITH: Seafood, chicken, salad, fruit, bread, pasta, desserts, in baking

VINEGAR PAIRINGS: Coconut, Peach, Apricot, Oregano, Cranberry Pear, Blackberry Ginger, Black Cherry, Pomegranate, Raspberry, Strawberry, Blueberry, Tangerine, Lavender

## Persian Lime

DESCRIPTION: Whole, fresh Persian limes with olives crushed together at the same time

PERFECT WITH: Seafood, chicken, salad, fruit, bread, pasta, desserts, in baking

VINEGAR PAIRINGS: Apricot, Coconut, Oregano, White, Pineapple, Tangerine, Lemongrass Mint, Blackberry Ginger, Cranberry Pear, Raspberry, Strawberry, Black Cherry, Pomegranate, Lavender

## Baklouti Green Chili

DESCRIPTION: Whole, fresh green chilies with olives crushed together at the same time

PERFECT WITH: Seafood, chicken, meat, vegetables, marinades or anything needing a punch of heat and spice

VINEGAR PAIRINGS: Peach, Pineapple, Honey Ginger, Cinnamon Pear, Dark Chocolate, Raspberry

# ⌒ WHOLE HERB FUSED OLIVE OIL ⌒

## Wild Rosemary

DESCRIPTION: Whole herb and olives crushed together at the same time — the perfect embodiment of heart and soul of rosemary

PERFECT WITH: Chicken, fish, meat, vegetables, salads, rice, potatoes, eggs

VINEGAR PAIRINGS: Cranberry Pear, Sicilian Lemon, Oregano, Peach, Pomegranate, Strawberry, Raspberry, Black Cherry, Fig

# ⌒ GOURMET OILS ⌒

## Roasted Walnut

DESCRIPTION: Walnuts slowly roasted in the traditional method, then expeller-pressed and lightly filtered

PERFECT WITH: Vegetables, salads, fruits, in baking

VINEGAR PAIRINGS: Champagne, Cinnamon Pear, Coconut, Blueberry, Dark Espresso, Fig, Maple, Pomegranate, Red Apple

## Roasted Sesame

DESCRIPTION: Roasted slow and low, then pressed in small batches

PERFECT WITH: Chicken, seafood, salads, soups, vegetables

VINEGAR PAIRINGS: Blackberry Ginger, Coconut, Pineapple

## White Truffle

DESCRIPTION: A smooth, unmistakable, intense white truffle flavor made in an artisan fashion without the use of any extracts

PERFECT WITH: Sauces, rice, risotto, vegetables

VINEGAR PAIRINGS: Fig, Sicilian Lemon

# FLAVORED DARK & WHITE
## BALSAMIC VINEGAR
# PAIRINGS

## BALSAMIC VINEGAR    PAIRINGS

*Apricot*
Garlic Olive Oil
Tuscan Herb Olive Oil
Eureka Lemon Olive Oil

*Black Cherry*
Butter Olive Oil
Chipotle Olive Oil
Eureka Lemon Olive Oil
Persian Lime Olive Oil
Tuscan Herb Olive Oil
Wild Rosemary Olive Oil

*Blackberry Ginger*
Tuscan Herb Olive Oil
Blood Orange Olive Oil
Eureka Lemon Olive Oil
Persian Lime Olive Oil
Roasted Sesame Oil

*Blueberry*
Blood Orange Olive Oil
Eureka Lemon Olive Oil
Basil Olive Oil
Roasted Walnut Oil

*Champagne*
Herbes de Provence Olive Oil
Tarragon Olive Oil
Tuscan Herb Olive Oil
Garlic Olive Oil
Roasted Walnut Oil

## Cinnamon Pear

Basil Olive Oil
Butter Olive Oil
Chipotle Olive Oil
Wild Mushroom and Sage Olive Oil
Blood Orange Olive Oil
Roasted Walnut Oil
Baklouti Olive Oil

## Coconut

Butter Olive Oil
Chipotle Olive Oil
Cilantro and Roasted Onion Olive Oil
Blood Orange Olive Oil
Eureka Lemon Olive Oil
Persian Lime Olive Oil
Roasted Sesame Oil
Roasted Walnut Oil

## Cranberry Pear

Herbes de Provence Olive Oil
Tuscan Herb Olive Oil
Blood Orange Olive Oil
Eureka Lemon Olive Oil
Persian Lime Olive Oil

## Dark Chocolate

Chipotle Olive Oil
Blood Orange Olive Oil
Tuscan Herb Olive Oil
Baklouti Olive Oil
Roasted Walnut Oil

## Fig

Basil Olive Oil
Cilantro and Roasted Onion Olive Oil
Garlic Olive Oil
Tuscan Herb Olive Oil
Wild Mushroom and Sage Olive Oil
Blood Orange Olive Oil
Wild Rosemary Olive Oil
Roasted Walnut Oil
White Truffle Oil

## Grapefruit

Basil Olive Oil
Garlic Olive Oil
Herbes de Provence Olive Oil

**Honey Ginger**
- Chipotle Olive Oil
- Cilantro and Roasted Onion Olive Oil
- Garlic Olive Oil
- Harissa Olive Oil
- Herbes de Provence Olive Oil
- Baklouti Olive Oil

**Jalapeño**
- Basil Olive Oil
- Chipotle Olive Oil
- Garlic Olive Oil
- Harissa Olive Oil

**Lavender**
- Herbes de Provence Olive Oil
- Eureka Lemon Olive Oil
- Persian Lime Olive Oil

**Lemongrass Mint**
- Cilantro and Roasted Onion Olive Oil
- Persian Lime Olive Oil

**Maple**
- Butter Olive Oil
- Chipotle Olive Oil
- Blood Orange Olive Oil
- Roasted Walnut Oil

**Oregano**
- Basil Olive Oil
- Garlic Olive Oil
- Eureka Lemon Olive Oil
- Persian Lime Olive Oil
- Wild Rosemary Olive Oil

**Peach**
- Chipotle Olive Oil
- Cilantro and Roasted Onion Olive Oil
- Herbes de Provence Olive Oil
- Tarragon Olive Oil
- Tuscan Herb Olive Oil
- Eureka Lemon Olive Oil
- Baklouti Olive Oil
- Wild Rosemary Olive Oil

### Pineapple

Basil Olive Oil
Blood Orange Olive Oil
Baklouti Olive Oil
Chipotle Olive Oil
Garlic Olive Oil
Roasted Sesame Oil
Tarragon Olive Oil
Harissa Olive Oil

### Pomegranate

Cilantro and Roasted Onion Olive Oil
Garlic Olive Oil
Herbes de Provence Olive Oil
Eureka Lemon Olive Oil
Persian Lime Olive Oil
Baklouti Olive Oil
Wild Rosemary Olive Oil
Roasted Walnut Oil

### Raspberry

Baklouti Olive Oil
Eureka Lemon Olive Oil
Basil Olive Oil
Herbes de Provence Olive Oil
Persian Lime Olive Oil
Tarragon Olive Oil
Blood Orange Olive Oil
Chipotle Olive Oil

### Red Apple

Cilantro and Roasted Onion Olive Oil
Wild Mushroom and Sage Olive Oil
Blood Orange Olive Oil
Roasted Walnut Oil

### Sicilian Lemon

Garlic Olive Oil
Herbes de Provence Olive Oil
Tuscan Herb Olive Oil
Wild Mushroom and Sage Olive Oil
Wild Rosemary Olive Oil
White Truffle Oil

**Strawberry**
Basil Olive Oil
Butter Olive Oil
Eureka Lemon Olive Oil
Persian Lime Olive Oil
Harissa Olive Oil
Wild Rosemary Olive Oil
Roasted Walnut Oil

**Tahitian Vanilla**
Blood Orange Olive Oil
Butter Olive Oil
Cilantro and Roasted Onion Olive Oil
Tuscan Herb Olive Oil
Wild Mushroom and Sage Olive Oil

**Tangerine**
Chipotle Olive Oil
Eureka Lemon Olive Oil
Persian Lime Olive Oil

**Traditional Style**
Any Ultra-Premium Extra-Virgin Olive Oil
Any Flavored Olive Oil

**White Premium**
Any Ultra-Premium Extra-Virgin Olive Oil
Any Flavored Olive Oil

# DESCRIPTIONS OF DARK & WHITE BALSAMIC VINEGARS

## Apricot

DESCRIPTION: Sweet, tart and crisp with a subtle aroma of honeysuckle

PERFECT WITH: Pork, fish, seafood, salad, fruit

OIL PAIRINGS: Garlic, Tuscan Herb, Eureka Lemon, Persian Lime

## Black Cherry

DESCRIPTION: Sweet, fragrant natural black cherry

PERFECT WITH: Beef, chicken, pork, salad, vegetables, ice cream, yogurt

OIL PAIRINGS: Butter, Chipotle, Tuscan Herb, Eureka Lemon, Persian Lime, Wild Rosemary

## Blackberry Ginger

DESCRIPTION: Sweet blackberries spiked with robust ginger

PERFECT WITH: Pork, chicken, seafood, salads, fruit, desserts

OIL PAIRINGS: Garlic, Tuscan Herb, Blood Orange, Eureka Lemon, Persian Lime, Roasted Sesame

## Blueberry

DESCRIPTION: Rich, flavorful, succulent blueberries

PERFECT WITH: Pork, beef, chicken, salad, fruit

OIL PAIRINGS: Blood Orange, Eureka Lemon, Roasted Walnut

# Champagne

DESCRIPTION: Dark Balsamic blended with sparkling white French Champagne vinegar; acidity 6%

PERFECT WITH: Salads, pork

OIL PAIRINGS: Garlic, Herbes de Provence, Tarragon, Tuscan Herb, Roasted Walnut

# Cinnamon Pear

DESCRIPTION: Spicy, warm flavor with the unique taste of d'anjou pear

PERFECT WITH: Seafood, pork, fruit, oatmeal, desserts

OIL PAIRINGS: Basil, Butter, Chipotle, Wild Mushroom and Sage, Baklouti, Roasted Walnut

# Coconut

DESCRIPTION: Creamy, tropical coconut flavor

PERFECT WITH: Seafood, chicken, pork, salad, fruit, soup, vegetables

OIL PAIRINGS: Butter, Chipotle, Cilantro and Roasted Onion, Blood Orange, Eureka Lemon, Persian Lime, Roasted Sesame, Roasted Walnut

# Cranberry Pear

DESCRIPTION: Tart, clean, crisp with a deep rose blush color

PERFECT WITH: Fish, salad, fruit, chicken, pork

OIL PAIRINGS: Herbes de Provence, Tuscan Herb, Blood Orange, Eureka Lemon, Persian Lime, Wild Rosemary

# Dark Chocolate

DESCRIPTION: Complex blend of three different chocolates with deep flavor

PERFECT WITH: Chicken, pork, beef, salads, fruit, desserts

OIL PAIRINGS: Chipotle, Blood Orange, Baklouti

## Dark Espresso

DESCRIPTION: Complex layering of authentic espresso and dark roasted coffee

PERFECT WITH: Scallops, steak, vegetables, salad, desserts

OIL PAIRINGS: Chipotle, Tuscan Herb, Blood Orange, Baklouti, Roasted Walnut

## Fig

DESCRIPTION: Bursting with natural fig flavor

PERFECT WITH: Salmon, lamb, beef, chicken, pork, salad, fruit, cheese, desserts

OIL PAIRINGS: Basil, Cilantro and Roasted Onion, Garlic, Tuscan Herb, Wild Mushroom and Sage, Blood Orange, Wild Rosemary, Roasted Walnut, White Truffle

## Grapefruit

DESCRIPTION: Crisp, clean, citrus flavor

PERFECT WITH: Seafood, chicken, pork, salads, rice, fruits

OIL PAIRINGS: Basil, Garlic, Herbes de Provence

## Honey Ginger

DESCRIPTION: Gentle, spicy heat of ginger with the subtle sweetness of honey

PERFECT WITH: Chicken, pork, seafood, salad, fruit, rice

OIL PAIRINGS: Chipolte, Cilantro and Roasted Onion, Garlic, Harissa, Herbes de Provence, Baklouti

## Jalapeño

DESCRIPTION: Sweet, spicy, tart with a slight touch of heat

PERFECT WITH: Chicken, pork, beef, salad, vegetables

OIL PAIRINGS: Basil, Chipotle, Garlic, Harissa

# Lavender

DESCRIPTION: Floral, sweet and elegant essence of lavender

PERFECT WITH: Lamb, pork, chicken, beef, salad, fruit, vegetables

OIL PAIRINGS: Herbes de Provence, Eureka Lemon, Persian Lime

# Lemongrass Mint

DESCRIPTION: Tart, crisp, clean flavors of Thai lemongrass and mint

PERFECT WITH: Seafood, dipping sauce, rice, pasta, salad

OIL PAIRINGS: Cilantro and Roasted Onion, Persian Lime

# Maple

DESCRIPTION: Infused with 100% pure Vermont maple syrup

PERFECT WITH: Meat, marinades, pork, dressings, fruit, ice cream, pancakes, oatmeal, root vegetables, desserts

OIL PAIRINGS: Butter, Chipotle, Blood Orange, Roasted Walnut

# Oregano

DESCRIPTION: Sharp, exquisite flavor of Mediterranean oregano

PERFECT WITH: Beef, chicken, fish, salad, tomatoes, cucumbers

OIL PAIRINGS: Basil, Garlic, Eureka Lemon, Persian Lime, Wild Rosemary

# Peach

DESCRIPTION: Crisp with a taste of peachy sweetness

PERFECT WITH: Seafood, fish, pork, salad, fruit

OIL PAIRINGS: Chipotle, Cilantro and Roasted Onion, Herbes de Provence, Tarragon, Tuscan Herb, Eureka Lemon, Baklouti, Wild Rosemary

# Pineapple

DESCRIPTION: Crisp with sweet ripe pineapple flavor
PERFECT WITH: Seafood, pork, salad, fruit
OIL PAIRINGS: Basil, Garlic, Harissa, Tarragon, Tuscan Herb, Blood Orange, Baklouti, Roasted Sesame

# Pomegranate

DESCRIPTION: Intense, sweet-tart pomegranate flavor
PERFECT WITH: Chicken, duck, beef, lamb, salad, fruit, pound cake
OIL PAIRINGS: Cilantro and Roasted Onion, Garlic, Herbes de Provence, Eureka Lemon, Persian Lime, Wild Rosemary, Roasted Walnut

# Raspberry

DESCRIPTION: Fresh, ripe raspberry flavor
PERFECT WITH: Chicken, pork, vegetables, salad, desserts
OIL PAIRINGS: Basil, Chipotle, Herbes de Provence, Garlic, Tarragon, Blood Orange, Eureka Lemon, Persian Lime, Baklouti, Wild Rosemary

# Red Apple

DESCRIPTION: Aroma and flavor of a delicate, sweet apple
PERFECT WITH: Poultry, pork, fruit, salad, desserts
OIL PAIRINGS: Cilantro and Roasted Onion, Wild Mushroom and Sage, Blood Orange, Roasted Walnut

# Sicilian Lemon

DESCRIPTION: Crisp lemon flavor and aroma with perfectly balanced acidity
PERFECT WITH: Seafood, pasta, salad, vegetables, fruit
OIL PAIRINGS: Garlic, Herbes de Provence, Tarragon, Tuscan Herb, Wild Mushroom and Sage, Wild Rosemary, White Truffle

# Strawberry

DESCRIPTION: Both sour and tart with a hint of sweetness

PERFECT WITH: Salad, fruit, desserts

OIL PAIRINGS: Basil, Butter, Harissa, Tuscan Herb, Eureka Lemon, Persian Lime, Wild Rosemary

# Tahitian Vanilla

DESCRIPTION: Sultry, fragrant Tahitian vanilla bean flavor

PERFECT WITH: Fruit, salads, desserts

OIL PAIRINGS: Butter, Cilantro and Roasted Onion, Tuscan Herb, Wild Mushroom and Sage, Blood Orange

# Tangerine

DESCRIPTION: Tart flavor made with whole fruit tangerine essence

PERFECT WITH: Fish, chicken, salad, vegetables, desserts

OIL PAIRINGS: Chipotle, Eureka Lemon, Persian Lime

# Traditional Style

DESCRIPTION: Rich, dense, 18 years old, 4% acidity, Four-Leaf Quality Equivalent Condimento

PERFECT WITH: Salads, vegetables, fruit, desserts

OIL PAIRINGS: any Ultra-Premium Extra-Virgin Olive Oil or any flavored olive oil

# White Premium

DESCRIPTION: Crisp, light, sweet, fruity and artfully balanced

PERFECT WITH: Fish, fruit, salad

OIL PAIRINGS: any Ultra-Premium Extra-Virgin Olive Oil or any flavored olive oil

# PART TWO
# RECIPES

# SMALL BITES

# Dipping Oil

Serves: 4

## ingredients

½ cup Ultra-Premium Extra-Virgin Olive Oil
1 clove garlic, thinly sliced
Traditional Dark Balsamic Vinegar, a drizzle
2-3 tablespoons Parmesan or Romano
cheese, grated
Red pepper flakes, a pinch
Salt and pepper to taste

## Method

Place Olive Oil in a shallow decorative bowl. Swirl a drizzle of Balsamic Vinegar in the center of the bowl. Add Olive Oil, red pepper flakes, salt, pepper and cheese.

Dipping Oils are fun to serve, are very versatile and are easy to put together. Any pure olive oil will work and most any flavored oil can be used, along with flavored balsamic vinegar, depending on the taste you're after. This is a good basic recipe.

## To Serve

Serve with crusty bread, such as Italian or French bread, cut into slices or cubes.

## Variations

* Try a flavored oil and balsamic vinegar, such as Tuscan Herb Olive Oil and Oregano Balsamic. See pairings for additional suggestions.

* Add complementary dried herbs for a new taste.

* Instead of bread, serve with cut-up vegetables, such as bell peppers, fennel, radicchio, lettuce, endive, or other substantial leafy green.

# Toasts with Olive Oil

Makes 2-3 slices per person

## ingredients

Large loaf of Italian or French bread, thickly sliced

3-4 cloves garlic, smashed

Ultra-Premium Extra-Virgin Olive Oil — enough to drizzle over the slices

Salt, course ground

## Method

Slice enough bread for the number of people serving. Grill or toast bread slices. Smash garlic clove and rub it on the bread until it covers the slice. Drizzle with robust Ultra-Premium Extra-Virgin Olive Oil.

This toasted bread, known as crostini in Italy, is a favorite in Italy and Spain and can be topped with a variety of foods or eaten on its own. It's so easy and simple to make, yet very versatile. This is an authentic recipe, but you can also experiment with this one, using different flavored oils each time!

## To Serve

Arrange on small platter and sprinkle a pinch of coarse ground salt. Serve with a glass of wine or cocktail.

## Variations

* Before drizzling the top with olive oil, cover the bread slice with creamy, pureed white beans, fresh chopped tomatoes, roasted red peppers, olive or eggplant puree, chorizo or anchovy.

* In Spain, after the toast is rubbed with garlic, a tomato is rubbed on the toast until nothing is left but the skin. This creates a subtle tomato flavor and is the base for different tapas.

* After the topping is placed, drizzle with the olive oil of your choice. Flavored oils work beautifully, such as Basil, Garlic, Tuscan Herb, Herbes de Provence, Eureka Lemon, and hot oils, such as Baklouti or Harissa Olive Oil.

# Roasted Red Pepper Caprese

Serves: 4

## Ingredients

1 jar of roasted red peppers, 12 ounces
2 cloves garlic, peeled and chopped
¼ cup Basil Olive Oil
4 ounces Feta cheese
2 tablespoons fresh chives, chopped
Salt and cracked pepper to taste

## Method

To avoid tearing, carefully remove roasted red peppers from jar. Drain well. Place peppers in a small bowl and cover with about half of the olive oil. Chop garlic and add to mixture, along with salt to taste. Gently mix so as not to break up the pepper pieces. Chop chives and cut 2 slices of feta for each serving.

Drizzle a small amount of Basil Olive Oil on a small salad plate. Place 2 slices of roasted red peppers over the olive oil, and top with 2 slices of feta cheese. Drizzle a little olive oil on top. Add salt and cracked pepper and drizzle with a little more olive oil. Sprinkle chives over top. Add a little more cracked pepper, as desired.

## To Serve

This is easier to serve if prepared on small individual plates.

## Variation

Try using peaches, mozzarella cheese and Tarragon Olive Oil, and fresh tarragon garnish. Makes for a sweet taste, with a hint of licorice-like flavor.

THIS IS *a tiny* DEPARTURE FROM TRADITIONAL TOMATO, MOZZARELLA AND BASIL CAPRESE AND TASTES JUST AS GOOD, IF NOT BETTER.

KEEP A BAG OF
FROZEN COOKED, PEELED
AND DEVEINED SHRIMP
IN THE FREEZER TO
HAVE ON HAND FOR
THIS TASTY, HEALTHY
APPETIZER. IF FRESH
MANGOES ARE NOT
AVAILABLE, FROZEN
MANGO CHUNKS WORK
FINE IN THIS RECIPE.

# Mango Shrimp Bites

Makes 24

## ingredients

½ pound cooked, peeled and deveined shrimp, chopped

½ mango, finely diced – about 1 cup

2 tablespoons fresh cilantro, chopped

2 tablespoons Ultra-Premium Extra-Virgin Olive Oil

1 tablespoon lime juice

2 teaspoons fresh ginger, grated

¼ teaspoon salt

Pepper to taste

24 endive leaves – about 3 small heads

## Method

Gently remove endive leaves and wash and allow to dry. Combine shrimp, mango, cilantro, olive oil, lime juice, ginger, salt and pepper. Spoon mixture into endive leaves. The shrimp mixture can be made about one hour before serving. Endive leaves should be filled no sooner than 30 minutes prior to serving.

## To Serve

Arrange endive leaves on serving platter and serve.

## Variations

* Cilantro and Roasted Onion and Persian Lime Olive Oil can be used to enhance the flavor.

* This dish also makes a delicious salad. Just chop up the endive into bite size pieces, combine the chopped shrimp and all other ingredients and toss and serve.

# Healthy Hummus

Serves: 4-6

## ingredients

2 cans garbanzo beans, drained – 15.5 ounce cans
⅓ cup Chipotle Olive Oil
⅓ cup lemon juice
2 tablespoons Roasted Sesame Oil
2 large cloves garlic, peeled
1 tablespoon cumin, ground
1 teaspoon salt or to taste

This is a simple recipe and can be whipped up in a few minutes. Keep the ingredients in your pantry for a last minute appetizer.

## Method

Place all ingredients into a food processor. Pulse until smooth.

## To Serve

Place in colorful bowl and serve with fresh or baked seasoned pita (see Lagniappe).

## Variations

* Use Garlic, Lemon or Lime Olive Oil instead of Chipotle and/or Roasted Sesame Oil.
* To make Roasted Red Pepper Hummus, use 2 cans garbanzo beans and add one jar roasted red peppers, drained.

# Last-Minute Layered Hummus

Serves: 4-6

## ingredients

8 ounces cream cheese, softened

8 ounces prepared hummus – your favorite brand and flavor – or hummus from opposite page

½ cucumber, seeded and chopped

Cavender's Greek Seasoning

Tuscan Herb Olive Oil to drizzle

## Method

Layer first three ingredients. Sprinkle with Cavender's Greek Seasoning. Drizzle with Tuscan Herb Olive Oil.

## To Serve

Place in serving bowl and serve with pita triangles.

For an even easier, quicker hummus, use prepared ingredients and you'll have this done in a flash. Cavender's Greek Seasoning contains a blend of salt, pepper, herbs and spices, and combined with Tuscan Herb Olive Oil makes this a tasty and super-quick appetizer.

MARINADES, DRESSINGS & REDUCTIONS

Marinades are simple ways to add flavor to any meat, fish, poultry or vegetable dish. Flavored oils and flavored balsamic vinegars make it easy to create marinades according to taste. Follow the basic recipe, substitute any of your favorites, and enjoy the results.

# Basil/Tarragon Marinade

Serves: 4

## ingredients

½ cup Basil Olive Oil
½ small yellow onion, roughly chopped
2 tablespoons Tarragon Olive Oil
¼ cup dry white wine

## Method

Place all ingredients in food processor or blender for 20 seconds. (Over-processing will change the texture and flavor.) Place poultry or fish in a glass baking dish and cover with marinade mixture. Cover and refrigerate for 20 minutes for fish, or 2–3 hours for chicken.

## to Serve

Remove chicken or fish from marinade and cook as desired. Discard marinade.

## Variations

Marinades can be made from most any Ultra-Premium or Extra-Virgin Flavored Olive Oils, Dark or White Balsamic Vinegars. Consult the Pairings pages for suggested combinations. For example, pairing Persian Lime Olive Oil and Coconut Balsamic Vinegar as a marinade for fish, particularly red snapper, makes for a delicious, tropical combination of flavors.

# Chipotle Grill Marinade

Serves: 4

## ingredients

½ cup Chipotle Olive Oil
3 fresh limes — squeeze ¼ cup juice — plus slices for garnish
1 tablespoon minced garlic
2 teaspoons salt
1 teaspoon pepper

## Method

Mix all ingredients and place in a large ziplock plastic bag with your favorite chicken, meat, seafood or vegetables. Refrigerate for at least 1 hour — longer if able — so flavors have a chance to soak in. When ready, remove food from marinade and grill or cook as desired. Discard marinade.

## to Serve

Place on serving platter and serve. Garnish with fresh lime slices.

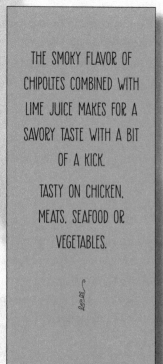

THE SMOKY FLAVOR OF CHIPOLTES COMBINED WITH LIME JUICE MAKES FOR A SAVORY TASTE WITH A BIT OF A KICK.

TASTY ON CHICKEN. MEATS. SEAFOOD OR VEGETABLES.

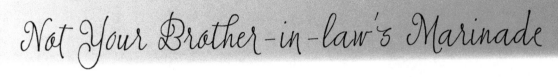

# Not Your Brother-in-law's Marinade

Serves: 4 (1½-2 pounds meat)

## ingredients

½ – 1 cup Ultra-Premium Extra-Virgin Olive Oil

Juice of 3-4 limes

4-5 cloves garlic, chopped

Handful fresh cilantro, chopped, plus a couple of sprigs for garnish

## Method

Place all ingredients in bowl and mix well. Rub all over meat and place in zip-lock bag. Refrigerate overnight. When ready to cook, remove meat from marinade. Discard marinade. Pat meat dry and place on grill. Add a good sprinkle of salt and pepper on both sides of the meat right before grilling – this is essential.

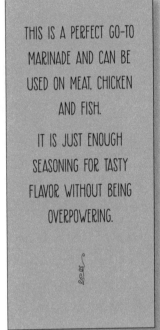

THIS IS A PERFECT GO-TO MARINADE AND CAN BE USED ON MEAT, CHICKEN AND FISH.

IT IS JUST ENOUGH SEASONING FOR TASTY FLAVOR WITHOUT BEING OVERPOWERING.

## To Serve

Slice meat and place on platter, garnishing with fresh cilantro.

## Variation

Try using any flavored olive oil, such as Persian Lime, Eureka Lemon, Garlic, Cilantro and Roasted Onion, Harissa, Baklouti or Chipotle Olive Oil, or your choice.

# Basic Vinaigrette

Though this is a basic recipe, there is nothing basic about its taste.
Using good quality, fresh Ultra-Premium Extra-Virgin Olive Oil
and aged Dark or White Balsamic Vinegar makes exceptional vinaigrette.

The typical proportion is 3 parts Olive Oil to 1 part Balsamic Vinegar, or
according to taste. Once you start making and using your own homemade
vinaigrette, you'll never go back to store-bought brands.

Makes 1 cup

## ingredients

¾ cup Ultra-Premium Extra-Virgin Olive Oil

¼ cup Traditional Dark Balsamic Vinegar

2 tablespoons water

½ teaspoon honey

1 large clove garlic, smashed

¾ teaspoon salt

⅛ teaspoon pepper

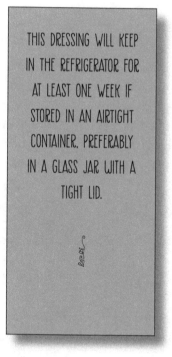

THIS DRESSING WILL KEEP
IN THE REFRIGERATOR FOR
AT LEAST ONE WEEK IF
STORED IN AN AIRTIGHT
CONTAINER, PREFERABLY
IN A GLASS JAR WITH A
TIGHT LID.

## Method

Peel garlic and smash. Place all ingredients in
glass jar with a tight lid. Shake well to blend.

## To Serve

If not using immediately, can be stored in the refrigerator. For optimum flavor
bring to room temperature before using.

## Variation

See Pairings pages for perfect flavored olive oil and flavored balsamic vinegar
combinations or make your own unique combinations.

# Cilantro and Roasted Onion and Raspberry Balsamic Vinaigrette

Makes ½ cup

## ingredients

4 tablespoons Cilantro and Roasted Onion Olive Oil

3 tablespoons Raspberry Balsamic Vinegar

1 clove garlic, minced

1 tablespoon honey

1 tablespoon Dijon mustard

Salt and pepper to taste

## Method

Place all ingredients in a jar with a tight lid and shake vigorously.

## To Serve

Gently pour and mix over fresh salad greens or drizzle over vegetables. If not using immediately, store in refrigerator in sealed container. Bring to room temperature before using.

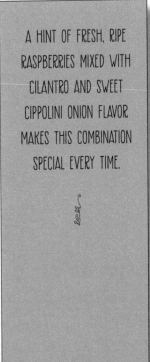

A HINT OF FRESH, RIPE RASPBERRIES MIXED WITH CILANTRO AND SWEET CIPPOLINI ONION FLAVOR MAKES THIS COMBINATION SPECIAL EVERY TIME.

Balsamic reductions, glazes, or simple syrups add so much flavor to any dish. The sweet-tangy combination is great on salads, as a finishing sauce for grilled chicken, fish, as a dip for veggies, or over ice cream and berries.

Use a non-reactive sauce pan, such as a stainless steel pan. Turn on the ventilation fan in your kitchen or open the window while doing reductions as the fragrance can be intense.

# Perfect Balsamic Vinegar Reduction Glaze

Makes ¾ cup

## Ingredients

1 cup Traditional Dark Balsamic Vinegar

## Method

Place balsamic vinegar in a small non-reactive saucepan over medium heat and bring to a boil. Reduce heat to low and let simmer for about 10 minutes until vinegar has reduced down. Watch this carefully as it can burn easily. When the vinegar coats the back of a spoon, you'll know it's done.

Remove from heat and let cool. If refrigerated, it may harden but can be placed in a bowl of warm water to soften.

## To Serve

Drizzle or spoon over your entrée, side or dessert.

## Variations

* Use any flavored dark balsamic of your choice for a unique glaze.
* For added flavor, you can also add a cinnamon stick, orange rind, whole peppercorns, rosemary sprig, or garlic cloves.

# Balsamic Syrup

Makes ¼ cup

## ingredients

⅔ cup Traditional Dark Balsamic Vinegar
1 tablespoon dark brown sugar, packed

## Method

In a non-reactive sauce pan, combine sugar and balsamic
vinegar. Boil over medium heat for about 3-4 minutes,
stirring using a wooden spatula. It is ready when it's
thickened and syrupy.

## To Serve

Cool before using. Can be stored in a sealed jar or container
in the refrigerator for about one month.

## Variation

May use any flavored Dark Balsamic Vinegar of your choice.

THIS IS A SIMPLE SYRUP
THAT CAN BE MADE
AHEAD OF TIME.

IT CAN BE ADDED TO
ROASTED VEGGIES AND
SALADS OR USED TO
BASTE MEATS.

# SALADS

# Grilled Bread Salad

Serves: 4

## ingredients

½ cup Ultra-Premium Extra-Virgin Olive Oil, plus a little extra if it seems dry

6 cloves garlic, crushed

4 cups crusty bread, cut into bite-size chunks 1" thick

1 cup red onion, diced ½-inch pieces

4 cups tomatoes, diced ½-inch pieces

3 tablespoons Premium White or Dark Balsamic Vinegar

1 bunch fresh basil leaves - save a few leaves for garnish

1 tablespoon capers

Salt and pepper to taste

## Method

Heat olive oil and sauté garlic 1-2 minutes. Add bread and sauté until golden brown. Lower heat and add onions and sauté another minute or so. Add the tomatoes and vinegar. Remove from heat. Add basil, capers and toss. If dry, add a little more olive oil.

## to Serve

Serve immediately. Garnish with whole basil leaves.

## Variations

* Experiment with this recipe by using flavored olive oils and flavored White or Dark Balsamic Vinegars. See pairings pages for suggestions.

* For a heartier salad, add 1-2 ounces of cheese, such as Parmigiano-Reggiano, Feta, Mozzarella or Manchego.

Bread salads are made many different ways all over the world, depending on the culture. Here is an easy recipe that can be modified using your desired flavored olive oil and balsamic vinegar. It's a great way to use leftover bread and much better for everyone instead of feeding it to the birds. It can be eaten alone or served with chicken, shrimp, tuna and vegetables, such as broccoli rabe or squash.

# Apricot and Arugula Salad

Serves: 4

## ingredients

¼ cup ricotta

½ teaspoon lemon zest, fine grated

1 tablespoon Apricot Balsamic Vinegar

¼ teaspoon Dijon mustard

4 teaspoons Eureka Lemon Olive Oil

3 cups baby arugula, lightly packed

3 medium apricots, cut into quarters

½ teaspoon salt

Pepper to taste

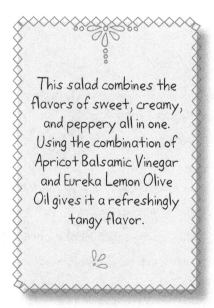

This salad combines the flavors of sweet, creamy, and peppery all in one. Using the combination of Apricot Balsamic Vinegar and Eureka Lemon Olive Oil gives it a refreshingly tangy flavor.

## Method

Combine ricotta, zest, ¼ teaspoon salt, pinch pepper in a small bowl and set aside. In another small bowl, combine vinegar, mustard, ¼ teaspoon salt, and whisk while drizzling in the olive oil.

Place arugula and apricots in a large bowl with about half of the dressing and toss gently. Taste and add more dressing, salt and pepper to taste, as needed.

## to Serve

Divide among 4 salad plates, spreading the salad on each plate. Drizzle with additional dressing. Top with ricotta mixture.

## Variations

* Try using Persian Lime instead of Eureka Lemon Olive Oil. It pairs nicely with Apricot Balsamic. Or experiment with your own pairing. See Pairings.

* You can use nectarines, peaches or plums instead of apricots. If there is extra ricotta mixture, it's delicious spread on a crostini or toast.

# Grilled Radicchio & Romaine Salad

Serves: 4

## ingredients

⅓ cup Ultra-Premium Extra-Virgin Olive Oil or flavored olive oil, such as Basil or Garlic Olive Oil

¼ cup Oregano Balsamic Vinegar

6 garlic cloves, chopped

½ teaspoon dried crushed red pepper flakes

4 large heads of radicchio, quartered lengthwise with some core still attached

1 medium head romaine lettuce, quartered lengthwise with some core still attached

1 cup Pecorino or Pecorino-Romano cheese, shaved

Salt to taste

Cracked pepper to taste

## Method

In large bowl, whisk Basil Olive Oil, Oregano Balsamic Vinegar, garlic, and crushed red pepper flakes. Add radicchio and romaine and toss to coat. Marinate 15 minutes. Prepare grill for a medium heat. Drain marinade into small bowl and set aside. Place radicchio and romaine on a grilling pan so it is not over a direct flame. Sprinkle with salt and pepper. Grill until edges are crisp and slightly charred, turning occasionally, about 6 minutes. Keep an eye on this, turning as needed. Remove from grill.

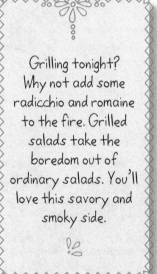

Grilling tonight? Why not add some radicchio and romaine to the fire. Grilled salads take the boredom out of ordinary salads. You'll love this savory and smoky side.

## To Serve

Separate radicchio and romaine from cores. Place on serving dish and drizzle with reserved marinade. Sprinkle with cheese shavings. Serve immediately.

## Variation

Use any flavored Olive Oil of your choice, such as Tuscan Herb, Basil, Garlic, Harissa, Herbes de Provence, Roasted Onion and Cilantro, Wild Rosemary or Wild Mushroom and Sage, to name a few. See Pairings for delicious combinations.

# Ruby Red Salad

Serves: 4

## ingredients

1 small head of red cabbage, chopped, reserving the whole outer leaves
2 oranges, sliced, peeled and chopped into bite size pieces
½ red onion, thinly sliced
1 mango or 1 papaya, peeled and cubed
¼ cup fresh cilantro, chopped, plus extra for garnish
Salt to taste

## Method

Combine all ingredients and mix thoroughly. Make salad dressing. Pour dressing over salad. Toss gently, coating everything well.

## To Serve

Place the dressed salad in a colorful bowl and serve. Garnish with cilantro. Or use the outer cabbage leaves as a liner for the bowl, or make individual servings, using a cabbage leaf for each serving. Either way, you'll have an attractive presentation.

## Variation

Try nectarines or peaches, a squeeze of lemon, even a few sliced radishes for a tasty variation.

This salad will perk up any meal, no matter the season. Its bright red color is cheerful and uplifting. And, it can be easily modified according to the season and availability of fresh fruits.

# Salad Dressing

## Ingredients

¾ cup Ultra Premium Extra-Virgin Olive Oil, or Blood Orange, Eureka Lemon, or Persian Lime Olive Oil

¼ cup Premium White Balsamic Vinegar or Sicilian Lemon, Peach, or Pineapple Balsamic Vinegar

## Method

Combine olive oil and vinegar of choice in a container with a tight lid and shake vigorously. Pour over salad, mixing thoroughly. If there is leftover dressing, store in refrigerator in a sealed container.

# Sensational Tomato Peach Salad

Serves: 4

## ingredients

4 ripe peaches, sliced

4 ripe tomatoes, quartered

4 ounces Feta cheese, crumbled — or more depending on taste

½ cup red onion, chopped

¼ cup pecans, chopped

Handful fresh mint, chopped, plus a few sprigs for garnish

Handful fresh basil, chopped, plus a few sprigs for garnish

Ultra-Premium Extra-Virgin Olive Oil to dress or flavored olive oil, such as Blood Orange

Salt to taste

This is a perfect summer salad and can be served with any meal, including brunch.

If the fruit is out of season, sprinkle a pinch of sugar on the peaches and a pinch of salt on the tomatoes to help bring out their flavors.

## Method

In a large bowl, combine peach slices and tomato quarters. Add feta cheese, red onion, pecans and olive oil and gently mix. Add mint and basil and gently toss.

## To Serve

Place on individual serving dishes and drizzle with a little more olive oil. Garnish with fresh mint or basil.

## Variations

* Try nectarines, plums or apricots instead of peaches.

* Use flavored olive oils, such as Blood Orange or Persian Lime Olive Oil.

# Crunchy Kale Salad

Serves: 4

## Ingredients

1 bunch kale, wash, remove tough stems and chop. Or use 1 bag, 10 ounces, prewashed and cut kale

¼ small head red cabbage, chopped

1 cup nuts, toasted and chopped, such as cashews, walnuts, sunflower seeds

2 medium carrots, peeled and grated

1 tablespoon Ultra-Premium Extra-Virgin Olive Oil

Salt to taste

## Method

Combine all ingredients in a large bowl. Massage kale and cabbage until they start to soften. Set aside. Make dressing.

> This is just one of the many ways kale can be fixed. This salad holds up well and can be stored in the refrigerator and eaten over a few days. Make enough to have for several meals.

# Kale Dressing

## Ingredients

1 apple, diced

2 cloves garlic

¼ cup Herbes de Provence Olive Oil

2 teaspoons honey

1 ½ tablespoons Pomegrante Balsamic Vinegar

1 teaspoon curry powder or turmeric powder

## Method

Place all dressing ingredients in a food processor. Blend until smooth.

## To Serve

Gently pour over salad and toss. Let marinate for 30 minutes before serving.

## Variation

Try adding Eureka Lemon Olive Oil for a lighter taste. See Pairings for additional pairing suggestions.

# PASTA

# Spaghetti with Olive Oil

Serves: 4

## Ingredients

1 pound spaghetti, cooked al dente

¼ cup Ultra-Premium Extra-Virgin Olive Oil or flavored Olive Oil

10 cloves garlic, thinly sliced

1 teaspoon red pepper flakes, dried

½ cup fresh parsley, chopped, plus a couple of sprigs for garnish

Parmigiano-Reggiano cheese, grated

## Method

In a small sauce pan, heat Olive Oil over a medium heat. Saute garlic until just soft – about 2 minutes. Add salt, pepper, red pepper flakes and ¼ cup chopped parsley. Mix, cover and remove from heat.

Cook spaghetti al dente according to package directions, reserving ¼ cup pasta water. Drain pasta.

## To Serve

Place spaghetti in serving bowl. Add olive oil and toss. If dry, add a little pasta water and coat spaghetti well. Top with remaining chopped parsley. Garnish with parsley sprigs. Serve immediately. Place grated cheese on table for individual use.

This is a traditional Italian dish that's easy to make and oh so tasty.

Use a robust Ultra-Premium Extra-Virgin olive oil for an intense flavor. Or, try a flavored olive oil for an herbaceous taste. Be sure to plate and serve this dish immediately because it dries out very quickly.

## Variations

* You can use angel hair, linguini, or cappellini for this dish.

* Try flavored olive oils, such as Basil, Garlic, Herbes de Provence, Wild Rosemary, Wild Mushroom and Sage, Butter, Eureka Lemon, or Tuscan Herb Olive Oil. For added heat, use Harissa or Baklouti Olive Oil.

# Cappellini with Scallops

Serves: 4

## ingredients

¾– 1 pound bay or sea scallops

½ cup flour

2 tablespoons Ultra-Premium Extra-Virgin Olive Oil for searing scallops

4 tablespoons Eureka Lemon Olive Oil

1 lemon, zested and juiced

1 pound cappellini, cooked al dente

⅓ cup fresh flat-leaf parsley, chopped, plus 3–4 stems for garnish

Salt and pepper to taste

This dish takes just a few minutes to prepare. Scallops need to be cooked a very short time to preserve their flavor. You can use any long, thin pasta, such as spaghetti or linguini. It even tastes good over orzo pasta.

## Method

If using bay scallops, leave whole. If using sea scallops, cut into quarters. In a large bowl, combine flour, salt and pepper. Dust scallops in flour mixture. In a skillet using high heat, add Ultra-Premium Extra-Virgin Olive Oil and heat for about 20–30 seconds. Place scallops in skillet to sear, turning when necessary – no more than 1–2 minutes each side. Add lemon juice and remove from heat and cover.

Cook cappellini al dente according to package directions. Drain and reserve ¼ cup pasta water.

## To Serve

Place pasta in large serving bowl. Add Eureka Lemon Olive Oil, scallops and toss. If dry, add pasta water and toss again. Top with lemon zest and chopped parsley. Garnish with parsley sprigs. Serve immediately.

## Variations

* Try this recipe using Eureka or Persian Lime Olive Oil (or a combination of both). Garlic or Harissa Olive Oil can be used for a hot-cha-cha flavor.

* Tuscan Herb, Herbes de Provence, Basil or Tarragon Olive Oil all work well with this dish.

* Instead of pasta, try serving over rice.

# You're a Gourmet Chef Pasta

Serves: 4

## ingredients

3 long carrots, sliced into thin slices

3 long zucchini, sliced into thin slices

6 ounces fresh mushrooms, sliced

2 tablespoons Herbes de Provence Olive Oil, plus a little extra for drizzling

2 tablespoons Butter Olive Oil

6 garlic cloves, minced

1 pound wide pasta, such as fettuccine or pappardelle

1 tablespoon fresh thyme leaves, chopped, and 2 sprigs for garnish

Salt and pepper to taste

(photo by Michele Senac)

## Method

Using a potato peeler, slice carrots and zucchini creating long, thin slices. Mince garlic. In a large skillet over medium heat, place Herbes de Provence Olive Oil and mushrooms and sauté. After a few minutes, add minced garlic, carrots, zucchini, salt and pepper and stir gently about 2–3 minutes. Watch carefully as you don't want the vegetables to overcook.

Cook pasta al dente, according to package directions. Drain.

This dish is colorful and pretty. Placed on a colorful patterned dish, the colors of the zucchini, mushrooms and carrots come to life.

## To Serve

Place pasta on a platter and toss with Butter Olive Oil. Add vegetables and toss gently. Top with chopped thyme. Drizzle a little Herbes de Provence Olive Oil on top and garnish with thyme sprigs. Serve immediately.

## Variations

* You can use pure Ultra-Premium Extra-Virgin Olive Oil instead of flavored olive oil.
* Or, try a variety of flavored oils, such as Wild Mushroom and Sage, Wild Rosemary, Cilantro and Roasted Onion Experiment with flavored oils and create your own signature dish.

# Not Your Mama's Mac and Cheese

Serves: 4-6

## Ingredients

1 pound elbow macaroni, cooked al dente

2 tablespoons White Truffle Olive Oil

4 tablespoons unsalted butter or ¼ cup Butter Olive Oil

4 tablespoons flour

2 cups whole milk, warmed

½ teaspoon cayenne pepper

¾ cup Fontina cheese, grated

¾ cup Gruyere cheese, grated

¾ cup Cheddar cheese, extra sharp, grated

¼ cup Parmesan cheese, grated

½ cup bread crumbs

Salt and pepper to taste

## Method

Preheat oven to 350°. Cook pasta al dente according to package directions. While pasta is cooking, heat butter or Butter Olive Oil over medium heat in a saucepan. Whisk in flour to create a roux for the white-sauce base. Simmer flour and butter over low heat for 5-7 minutes, then add warm milk in a steady stream, stirring, and simmer for 10 additional minutes. Do not allow to boil. Add salt, pepper, cayenne and all the cheeses except the Parmesan cheese. Stir for 2 minutes until cheese melts.

Drain pasta and place in oiled baking dish or large casserole. Pour cheese sauce over pasta and sprinkle top with bread crumbs and Parmesan cheese. Bake 15 minutes or until top is browned and crusty. Let rest for 10 minutes, then drizzle top with White Truffle Oil.

## To Serve

Serve from baking dish while it's nice and hot.

(Photo by Michele Senac)

## Variation

Try this with Chipotle, Wild Mushroom and Sage or Garlic Olive Oil, or any flavored olive oil of your choice.

White Truffle Oil is a connoisseur's olive oil made in an artisan fashion without the use of any extracts. It is smooth with an intense white truffle flavor. A little goes a long way.

Many of us grew up on mac and cheese, yet this is definitely not your mother's mac and cheese!

# Lemon Linguini

Serves: 6

## ingredients

1 pound linguini
⅔ cup Eureka Lemon Olive Oil
⅔ cup Parmesan cheese, grated
2 fresh lemons, zested and juiced for ⅓ cup juice, plus extra for garnish
¾ teaspoon salt, and to taste
½ teaspoon ground pepper, and to taste
⅓ cup fresh basil, chopped
⅓ cup fresh flat-leaf parsley, chopped, plus extra sprigs for garnish

## Method

In a large bowl, whisk oil, cheese, lemon juice, ¾ teaspoon salt, ½ teaspoon pepper until well-blended. Set aside. Cook linguine al dente, according to package directions. Drain, reserving 1 cup of cooking water. Add linguini to lemon sauce, along with basil, parsley and lemon zest. Toss gently, adding enough cooking water a little at a time to moisten. Add salt and pepper to taste.

## to Serve

Place in colorful serving bowl or on a platter. Sprinkle top with parsley and garnish with lemon slices. Serve immediately. Parmesan cheese can be placed on the table for individual use.

The lemon sauce can be made up to 8 hours prior to serving. Store in refrigerator and bring to room temperature before using.

This lemony pasta is so light it can be served as a simple supper or as a side with seafood.

(Photo by Michele Senac)

# Variations

* Any pasta can be used, such as spaghetti, angel hair,
cappellini, or penne.

* For a twist, try using Herbes de Provence, Tuscan Herb,
Garlic, Butter, Wild Mushroom, or Basil Olive Oil in this recipe.

# Sesame Pasta Salad

Serves: 6

## ingredients

1 pound linguine, broken in half

2 tablespoons Roasted Sesame Oil

3 tablespoons Ultra Premium Extra-Virgin Olive Oil

3 tablespoons honey

3 tablespoons soy sauce

3 tablespoons Honey Ginger Balsamic Vinegar

¼ teaspoon cayenne pepper

3 red bell peppers, seeded, thinly sliced

3 cups snow peas or sugar snap peas, sliced on bias

1 large red onion, thinly sliced

¾ cup honey-roasted peanuts, coarsely chopped, plus a few whole peanuts for garnish

½ cup fresh basil, chopped, plus extra for garnish

1 teaspoon salt

## Method

Break pasta in half and cook al dente, according to package directions. Drain well, rinse with cold water and transfer to large bowl. Whisk together 1 tablespoon Roasted Sesame Oil, honey, soy sauce, Honey Ginger Balsamic Vinegar, cayenne pepper and salt in small bowl. Start out with a couple of tablespoons of Sesame Oil and taste as you go. If you want additional sesame flavor, you can always add more. Mix half of the dressing into the pasta. Heat Ultra-Premium Extra-Virgin Olive Oil in skillet over medium-high heat and add bell peppers, peas and onions, and sauté until just beginning to wilt, about 2 minutes. Do Not Overcook! Remove from heat. Add salt, peanuts and basil. Combine all ingredients with pasta, mixing gently while adding the remaining dressing to coat all the ingredients.

## to Serve

Place on large serving platter, garnish with fresh basil and honey-roasted peanuts. Can serve immediately or refrigerate until ready to serve. Serve at room temperature.

(Photo by Clare Hilger)

## Variations

* Use Asian soba noodles, found in most grocery stores, instead of linguini.

* Instead of Honey Ginger, try Lemongrass Mint or Coconut Balsamic Vinegar.

* If you want to spice it up, use Harissa Olive Oil instead of Roasted Sesame and omit the cayenne pepper because the Harissa will make it plenty hot enough!

* Try using fresh cilantro and/or fresh mint instead of fresh basil, or a combination of all three.

This delicious salad lends itself very well to using several different flavored oils and balsamic vinegars. It makes a great potluck dish. It can be served as a side or as a main dish with the addition of cooked chicken or shrimp. Roasted Sesame Oil is very flavorful and a little goes a long way.

# POTATOES, RICE & GRAINS

# Extra-Special Smashed Potatoes

Serves 6-8

## ingredients

3 pounds red potatoes, cut into large cubes

2 sprigs fresh rosemary, divided

2 garlic cloves, minced

1 tablespoon salt, divided

4 tablespoons Ultra-Premium Extra-Virgin Olive Oil, or flavored Olive Oil

2 tablespoons White Truffle Olive Oil, plus a few drops for serving

½ cup half-and-half

Ground pepper to taste

## Method

Cut potatoes in large cubes and rinse well. Place in large saucepan and cover with water. Remove the leaves from half of one of the rosemary sprigs, then place the sprigs into the water. Add minced garlic and 1 teaspoon salt. Bring potatoes to a boil, then reduce heat and simmer until potatoes are soft – usually about 15 minutes. Drain and remove the rosemary sprigs. Place potatoes in a large bowl.

Mince the remaining rosemary leaves. Add rosemary, Ultra-Premium Extra-Virgin Olive Oil, White Truffle Oil, half-and-half, salt, and pepper. Using a fork or potato masher, mash the potatoes in the saucepan until all ingredients are well combined and potatoes have reached desired consistency.

SMASHED OR MASHED, WHO DOESN'T LOVE THE TASTE OF POTATOES?

THE ADDED FLAVOR OF WHITE TRUFFLE OIL PUTS THIS ON THE LIST FOR THE ULTIMATE COMFORT FOODS!

## to Serve

Place in colorful serving bowl, drizzle a little extra White Truffle Oil on top. Serve warm.

## Variation

Substitute Garlic, Tarragon, Wild Rosemary, or Wild Mushroom and Sage for the Ultra-Premium Extra-Virgin Olive Oil.

# St. Simon's Sweet Potatoes

Serves: 4

## ingredients

2 pounds sweet potatoes, peeled and cubed into 2-inch cubes

1 red onion, chopped

2 cloves garlic, minced

¼ cup Tuscan Herb Olive Oil

Salt and pepper to taste

## Method

Preheat oven to 400°. In a large bowl, place potatoes, onions, garlic, Tuscan Herb Olive Oil, salt and pepper. Mix well, coating all ingredients with olive oil. Spread potatoes on a large baking dish. Roast for 1 hour 20 minutes, turning potatoes a couple of times so they roast evenly.

## to Serve

Place on serving dish and serve immediately.

SWEET POTATOES ARE SO HEALTHY AND BAKING THEM USING FLAVORED OLIVE OIL INCREASES THEIR TASTINESS. THE BLEND OF HERBS IN TUSCAN HERB OLIVE OIL IS THE PERFECT ACCOMPANIMENT. YOU'LL BE BLESSING ST. SIMON AND THIS DELICIOUS DISH RIGHT DOWN TO THE LAST POTATO.

## Variations

\* For a change, try a sweet Vidalia onion instead of the red onion.

\* Use Blood Orange Olive Oil for a sweet flavor or Rosemary Olive Oil for a flavor twist. Add chopped, fresh mint before baking for additional color and taste.

# Spicy Rice

Serves: 4

## ingredients

1 cup rice, uncooked
1 teaspoon Roasted Sesame Oil
¾ cup carrots, peeled and diced
½ cup onion, diced
2 cloves garlic, minced
2 cans chicken broth – 10.5 ounce cans
½ teaspoon curry powder
¼ teaspoon salt
⅛ teaspoon cayenne pepper

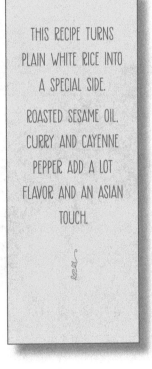

THIS RECIPE TURNS PLAIN WHITE RICE INTO A SPECIAL SIDE.

ROASTED SESAME OIL, CURRY AND CAYENNE PEPPER ADD A LOT FLAVOR AND AN ASIAN TOUCH.

## Method

Sauté carrots, onions, garlic in Roasted Sesame Oil until tender. Add broth, curry, salt and cayenne pepper. Bring to boil and stir in rice. Reduce heat, cover and simmer 20 minutes.

## To Serve

Fluff rice. Place in serving bowl and serve warm.

## Variations

* Orzo can be substituted for rice.

* To spice this up even more, try adding a little Harissa or Baklouti Olive Oil while sautéing the vegetables.

WILD RICE IS
ALWAYS A TREAT.

THIS EASY RECIPE CAN
BE MADE AHEAD OF
TIME AND REFRIGERATED.
IT TASTES BEST SERVED
AT ROOM TEMPERATURE.
USING FLAVORED OLIVE OIL
AND BALSAMIC VINEGAR
COMPLEMENTS WILD RICE
SO WELL AND ADDS TO
ITS DELICIOUS, NUTRITIOUS
TASTE.

# Cranberry Wild Rice

Serves: 4

## ingredients

1 cup wild rice

½ cup dried cranberries

½ cup slivered almonds

1 orange, sliced, peeled and cut into small pieces, or 1 can Mandarin oranges –
11 ounces, drained. Reserve a couple of orange slices or Mandarin oranges
for garnish

2 tablespoons Wild Mushroom and Sage Olive Oil

¼ cup Cranberry Pear Balsamic Vinegar

## Method

Cook wild rice according to package directions. Combine all ingredients, mix well,
cover and refrigerate.

## To Serve

Remove from refrigerator about 20 minutes prior to serving. Place in serving bowl
and garnish with orange slices or Mandarin oranges.

## Variations

* For a fruitier flavor, use Blood Orange Olive Oil. It pairs well with Cranberry
Pear Balsamic Vinegar.

* For an herbaceous taste, use Wild Rosemary Olive Oil. It pairs well with
Cranberry Pear Balsamic Vinegar.

# Quinoa with Chickpeas and Avocado

Serves: 4

## ingredients

1 cup grape tomatoes, quartered

1 can garbanzo beans, 15 ounces, rinsed and drained

1 cup cooked quinoa with 2 tablespoons Persian Lime Olive Oil

2 tablespoons red onion, finely chopped

1 tablespoon fresh cilantro, chopped, plus a few sprigs for garnish

1½ fresh limes, juiced – zest 1 lime for garnish

1 cup cucumber, peeled and diced

1 medium avocado, diced

Salt and pepper to taste

## Method

Cook quinoa according to package directions, adding 2 tablespoons Persian Lime Olive Oil to the water. Combine all ingredients, except avocado and cucumber, and refrigerate if not serving right away. Add cucumber and avocado just before serving and mix gently.

> THIS RECIPE PACKS IN THE PROTEIN. IT CAN BE SERVED AS A SIDE OR AS AN ENTRÉE FOR LUNCH OR SUPPER.

## to Serve

After adding cucumber and avocado, place in serving bowl, and sprinkle lime zest over the top. Garnish with cilantro leaves. Serve immediately.

## Variation

Using Cilantro and Roasted Onion Olive Oil will add a nutty flavor.

(Photo by Jackie Willey)

# Tasty Tabouleh

Serves: 6

## Ingredients

2 cups cooked bulgur wheat

½ cup Ultra-Premium Extra-Virgin Olive Oil or flavored Olive Oil

2 fresh lemons, juiced

½ cup fresh parsley, chopped

½ cup tomato, peeled and diced

2 tablespoons fresh mint, chopped, plus sprigs for garnish.

Salt and pepper to taste

## Method

Combine everything together in a large bowl. Toss and taste. Correct seasoning if needed. You may need to add more salt or extra mint or parsley, according to your taste. Cover and let sit for about 1 hour before serving.

## To Serve

Place in serving bowl and garnish with fresh mint.

## Variations

* Some recipes suggest peeled, chopped cucumber be added for a lighter flavor.

* Try flavored olive oils, such as Eureka Lemon, Garlic, Cilantro and Roasted Onion, Garlic or Basil Olive Oil for a unique and tasty flavor. A dash of Harissa or Baklouti Olive Oil will give it a little kick.

BE SURE TO FOLLOW THE PACKAGE DIRECTIONS FOR COOKING BULGUR WHEAT. IT TENDS TO EASILY OVERCOOK AND TURNS MUSHY IF TOO MUCH LIQUID IS USED. TABOULEH IS NUTRITIOUS AND REFRESHING AND CAN BE SERVED AS A SIDE, AN APPETIZER, A SALAD OR ADDED TO A SANDWICH.

MEAT

# I Love NY Strip Steak

Serves: 4

## ingredients

4 New York strip steaks or filets

Salt and pepper to taste

8 ounces blue cheese, crumbled

2 tablespoons dark chocolate sauce, prepared, or Dark Chocolate Balsamic Vinegar reduction (see Variation)

1 cup Dark Espresso Balsamic Vinegar

2 tablespoons butter

## Method

Season meat with salt and pepper. Grill steaks 10–12 minutes or until desired doneness. During the last 3 minutes of grilling, sprinkle blue cheese over steaks. Remove from grill and allow meat to rest for 5 minutes before serving.

Meanwhile, in a small non-reactive saucepan, combine 1 cup Dark Espresso Balsamic Vinegar with 2 tablespoons dark chocolate sauce. Bring to boil, reduce heat to low. Simmer uncovered until reduced by half, stirring occasionally. Remove from heat, add 2 tablespoons butter and stir to melt.

## to Serve

Drizzle sauce over steaks and serve immediately.

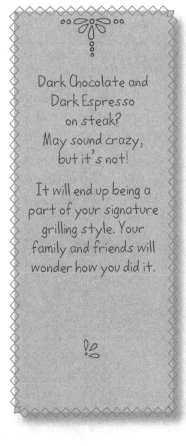

Dark Chocolate and Dark Espresso on steak? May sound crazy, but it's not!

It will end up being a part of your signature grilling style. Your family and friends will wonder how you did it.

## Variation

Omit the prepared dark chocolate sauce and make a chocolate reduction using 1 cup Dark Chocolate Balsamic Vinegar and 2 tablespoons butter. Delicious!

# Peppery Grilled Flank Steak

Serves: 4-6

## ingredients

1 ½ pounds flank steak

⅓ cup Traditional Dark Balsamic Vinegar

2 tablespoons Ultra-Premium Extra-Virgin Olive Oil

1 tablespoon + 1 teaspoon cracked pepper

2 teaspoons brown sugar

1 teaspoon garlic salt

## Method

Trim excess fat from steak. Score meat diagonally across grain at ¾-inch intervals. Place steak in shallow baking dish. Combine all ingredients and pour over steak. Cover and marinate in refrigerator for several hours, turning occasionally.

Remove steak from marinade and discard marinade. Grill over hot coals 8 minutes on each side or as desired. Or roast in 400° oven for 10 minutes. Check after 10 minutes and if not done, continue to roast a few more minutes, as desired

This lean cut really benefits from the tenderizing effects of a marinade. You'll love the simplicity of this one.

## To Serve

Slice steak diagonally across the grain into thin slices and place on platter. Serve immediately.

## Variations

* Blackberry Ginger, Honey Ginger or Fig Balsamic Vinegar are all great with flank steak.

* Additionally, you can add chopped onions to the top of the meat before grilling or roasting.

# Georgia Lamb Chops

Serves: 4

## ingredients

1 American rack of lamb (8 chops) or 2 New Zealand racks of lamb (16 chops) butter-flied

⅓–½ cup Ultra-Premium Extra-Virgin Olive Oil

4 medium sprigs fresh rosemary plus 2 large sprigs for garnish

Salt and pepper to taste

## Method

Preheat oven 400°. Place lamb in roasting pan and brush olive oil liberally on chops. Sprinkle with salt and pepper and add rosemary sprigs. Bake for 25–30 minutes. To be sure they are not over cooking, remove one chop at the end and check for doneness.

## To Serve

Place on serving platter and garnish with fresh rosemary. Serve immediately

## Variation

Have fun with this recipe by trying different flavored olive oils such as Wild Mushroom and Sage, Eureka Lemon, or Wild Rosemary Olive Oil.

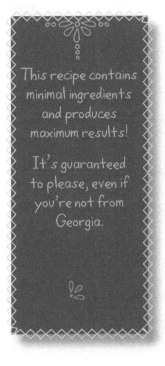

This recipe contains minimal ingredients and produces maximum results!

It's guaranteed to please, even if you're not from Georgia.

# Lamb Chops with Fig Balsamic Reduction

Serves: 4

## ingredients

4 lamb chops, ¾-inch thick

¾ teaspoon fresh rosemary, plus 2–3 sprigs for garnish

¼ teaspoon basil, dried

3 cloves garlic, minced

Salt and ground black pepper to taste

1 tablespoon Ultra-Premium Extra-Virgin Olive Oil – mild to medium intensity

¼ cup shallots, minced

⅓ cup Fig Balsamic Vinegar

¾ cup chicken broth

1 tablespoon butter or ¾ tablespoon Butter Olive Oil

¼ teaspoon salt

¼ teaspoon pepper

## Method

In a small bowl, combine rosemary, basil, garlic, salt and pepper. Rub mixture onto the lamb chops on both sides. Place on a plate, cover and set aside for 15–30 minutes so the flavors can be absorbed.

Heat olive oil in a large skillet over medium-high heat. Place the lamb chops in the skillet and cook for about 3 ½ minutes per side for medium rare, or continue to cook to as desired. Remove from the skillet, and keep warm on a serving platter.

Add shallots to the skillet, and sauté over medium-low heat for a few minutes, just until browned. Stir in Fig Balsamic Vinegar, scraping any bits of lamb from the bottom of the skillet, then stir in the chicken broth. Simmer and stir over medium-high heat for about 5 minutes or until sauce has reduced by half. Remove from heat and whisk in butter or Butter Olive Oil.

(Photo by Clare Hilger)

The combination of lamb and Fig Balsamic Vinegar will not only please lamb-lovers, but will have those who say they don't like lamb coming back for more.

## To Serve

Place lamb chops on serving platter and pour mixture over the chops. Sprinkle with additional salt and pepper and garnish with a couple of sprigs of fresh rosemary. Serve immediately.

## Variation

\* You can substitute Traditional Balsamic Vinegar for the Fig Balsamic Vinegar or use another of your favorite Dark Balsamic Vinegars, such as Pomegranate.

\* Substitute Wild Mushroom and Sage and Wild Rosemary Olive Oil or another favorite flavored olive oil instead of the Ultra-Premium Extra-Virgin Olive Oil.

# Crazy-Good Crock-Pot Pork Tenderloin

Serves: 6-8

## ingredients

Pork tenderloin, 2-3 pounds
⅓ cup Butter Olive Oil
½ cup Red Apple Balsamic Vinegar
¼ teaspoon cayenne pepper
1 teaspoon garlic, minced
Salt and pepper to taste

## Method

Place tenderloin in bottom of Crock-Pot®. In a separate bowl, mix all other ingredients and pour over tenderloin. Cover pot and cook on high for 1 hour. Reduce heat to low and cook an additional 3-4 hours. Remove tenderloin and discard liquid.

## To Serve

Place on platter and serve immediately.

## Variations

* Can be served shredded for wonderful barbeque sandwiches.
* Or use Honey Ginger Balsamic Vinegar or Traditional Dark Balsamic Vinegar for a savory flavor.

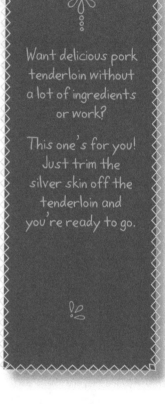

Want delicious pork tenderloin without a lot of ingredients or work?

This one's for you! Just trim the silver skin off the tenderloin and you're ready to go.

# Not Just For Chicks Chicken

Serves: 4

## ingredients

4 chicken quarters – bone-in, skin-on – or a combination of thighs and/or drumsticks

3 tablespoons Herbes de Provence Olive Oil + extra for drizzling

1 tablespoon Butter Olive Oil or 2 ¼ teaspoons butter

1 cup flour

1 lemon, cut in half plus lemon slices for garnish

2 shallots, peeled and halved lengthwise

¼ cup dry white wine

Salt and pepper to taste

## Method

Preheat oven to 375° and place Herbes de Provence Olive Oil and Butter Olive Oil or butter in a roasting pan and place in the oven.

> This is a simple dish that packs a lot of flavor. The combination of two flavored olive oils adds a fresh herbaceous taste. Even guys will love it.

In a paper or plastic bag, add flour and a pinch of pepper. Close and shake to mix the flour and pepper. Drop in a couple of pieces of chicken at a time and shake to coat thoroughly. Shake off any excess flour and continue until all the chicken pieces are coated.

Place coated chicken into roasting pan, cover with shallots, wine and lemon halves. Drizzle chicken with Herbes de Provence Olive Oil, salt and pepper. Bake for 20–25 minutes. Baste the chicken with the drippings and return to oven for another 15–20 minutes. Repeat the basting process one more time and bake for another 15 minutes or until the skin is crispy and golden brown.

## To Serve

Place chicken on a platter and garnish with lemon slices. Serve immediately.

## Variation

You can substitute other flavored olive oils such as Basil, Tuscan Herb, Eureka Lemon, Garlic, Wild Mushroom and Sage, Chipotle, Wild Rosemary and Harissa Olive Oil.

# Pork Tenderloin with Mushrooms and Fennel

Serves: 4-6

## ingredients

Pork tenderloin, 2 pounds

2 fennel bulbs, trimmed and cut into fourths, reserve fronds for garnish

3 large Portobello mushrooms, cut into fourths

¼ cup Wild Mushroom and Sage Olive Oil

2 tablespoons pepper, coarsely ground

½ teaspoon salt

½ cup Cinnamon Pear Balsamic Vinegar

1 cup whipping cream

## Method

Preheat oven 375°. Cut fennel and mushrooms and set aside. Brown tenderloin in 2 tablespoons Wild Mushroom and Sage Olive Oil over high heat for 4 minutes each side. Place in roasting pan fat side up and sprinkle with 1 tablespoon pepper and ¼ teaspoon salt. Add fennel and mushrooms. Drizzle with remaining Wild Mushroom and Sage Olive Oil. Roast for approximately 1 hour and 15 minutes. If using a meat thermometer, cook until internal temperature registers 130° for medium rare, and 145° for well done. Start checking temperature after about 30-45 minutes. Transfer to serving platter. Cover and set aside, letting it rest 20 minutes before carving.

Place roasting pan over cook top burners and add Cinnamon Pear Balsamic Vinegar and whisk to loosen browned bits from pan. Whisk in cream and remaining pepper. Bring to boil and simmer for a couple of minutes or until sauce is thickened.

## To Serve

Pour sauce over tenderloin, or place sauce in small serving bowl. Serve immediately.

## Variation

Substitute a sweet onion for the fennel and use
Cilantro and Roasted Onion Olive Oil instead of Wild
Mushroom and Sage Olive Oil.

Fennel and
mushrooms are
delicious fresh or
cooked.
Cooked with pork,
their flavors pop.

Take tenderloin
out of the
refrigerator about
1 hour before
roasting. Be sure
to trim the outer
silver skin. Using a
meat thermometer
is helpful, but not
essential.

# Apricot Balsamic Chicken

Serves: 4-6

## ingredients

2 pounds chicken breast tenderloins, cut into bite-sized pieces

½ cup Apricot Balsamic Vinegar

2 tablespoons Tuscan Herb Olive Oil

Salt and pepper to taste

1 white onion, chopped

3 tablespoons fresh, flat-leaf parsley, chopped

1 cup chicken stock

20 dried apricots or use a combination of 4 fresh apricots and 12 dried apricots

Using fresh and dried apricots adds to the beauty and taste of this dish. The Apricot Balsamic Vinegar brings out even more flavor.

Make it for the family or company, either way those at your table are bound to feel special.

## Method

Heat Tuscan Herb Olive Oil in a covered large skillet over medium-high heat. Season chicken with salt and pepper. Cook in hot oil until golden brown on the edges but still pink in the center – about 5 minutes. Stir in the onions and cook for about 3 minutes more. Pour in the Apricot Balsamic Vinegar and let simmer, allowing it to reduce for a few minutes. Cut half of the apricots in half, leaving the others whole. This includes both dried and fresh if using both. Add apricots and chicken stock. Cover and simmer over medium-low heat until apricots have softened – about 10-15 minutes.

## To Serve

Place on colorful serving platter and sprinkle with chopped parsley. Serve immediately.

## Variation

Garlic or Chipotle Olive Oil will give this dish a more intense flavor.

# SEAFOOD

# Roasted Shrimp and Orzo

Serves: 6

## ingredients

¾ pound orzo pasta

2 pounds shrimp, peeled and deveined – 16–18 count

½ cup Ultra-Premium Olive Oil plus extra for drizzling

½ cup fresh lemon juice – about 3 lemons

1 cup scallions, minced, using the white and green parts

1 cup fresh dill, chopped

1 cup fresh flat-leaf parsley, chopped, plus sprigs for garnish

1 cucumber, unpeeled, seeded, diced

½ cup red onion, diced

¾ pound feta cheese, diced

2 teaspoons salt, plus extra for sprinkling

1 teaspoon pepper, plus extra for sprinkling

Salt and pepper to taste

> YOU SAY, NOTHING BEATS SHRIMP AND RICE!
>
> HOW ABOUT SHRIMP AND ORZO PASTA? TRY THIS ONE AND YOU MAY CHANGE YOUR MIND.

## Method

Preheat oven 400°. Cook orzo pasta al dente according to package directions. Drain and place in large bowl. In a small bowl, whisk lemon juice, olive oil, salt and pepper to taste. Pour over pasta, mixing well. Place shrimp in baking dish and drizzle with olive oil and sprinkle with salt and pepper. Combine and place in single layer in dish. Roast 5–6 minutes until shrimp are cooked. Do Not Overcook!

Add the shrimp to the orzo. Then add scallions, dill, parsley, cucumber, onion, 2 teaspoons salt and 1 teaspoon pepper. Toss well. Add feta and stir gently. Allow to sit at room temperature 1 hour to allow the flavors to blend, or refrigerate overnight. Return to room temperature before serving.

## To Serve

Place on serving platter and garnish with fresh parsley sprigs.

## Variations

* Eureka Lemon and Persian Lime are wonderful flavor enhancers for this dish.

* If you're still not sure about orzo pasta, serve with rice.

# Simple Shrimp Scampi

Serves: 4

## ingredients

1 pound large shrimp, peeled and deveined

3-4 cloves garlic, finely chopped

2 shallots, finely chopped

3 tablespoons Eureka Lemon Olive Oil

2 tablespoons butter or 4 ½ tablespoons Butter Olive Oil

1 tablespoon chopped rosemary, plus 2-3 sprigs for garnish

1 tablespoon chopped parsley

1 tablespoon lemon juice, then quartered for garnish

Salt and pepper to taste

MAKING SCAMPI HAS NEVER BEEN EASIER.

USING BUTTER OLIVE OIL GIVES THIS DISH A LIGHT, BUTTERY FLAVOR..

## Method

Heat olive oil and butter in large sauté pan to medium heat. Add shallots and sauté until beginning to get soft. Add garlic and sauté lightly, but not brown. Add shrimp and turn up the heat, gently mixing and allowing the shrimp to sauté until they turn pink. Turn off heat and add rosemary, salt and pepper and mix.

(Photo by Sandy Burn)

## To Serve

Remove from heat and place on serving platter. Top with lemon juice and parsley. Garnish with lemon quarters and fresh rosemary sprigs. Serve immediately.

## Variations

* Eureka Lemon and Wild Rosemary Olive Oils were made for this dish!

* Try Chipotle, Harissa or Baklouti Olive Oil for a simple, spicy version.

# Savory Spiked Fish

Serves: 4

## ingredients

4 fish fillets, 4-6 ounces each
2 teaspoons dill
1 teaspoon Spike® Seasoning
½ cup Eureka Lemon Olive Oil
Ground pepper to taste

## Method

Place fish in covered baking dish – fillets not touching.
Drizzle with Eureka Lemon Oil, sprinkle with dill and Spike®
seasoning. Bake at 375° for 25-30 minutes.

## To Serve

Place on individual serving plates and serve immediately.

## Variations

* Persian Lime gives this dish a light citrus flavor.
* Baklouti Olive Oil will heat things up!

THIS IS A QUICK, EASY WAY TO COOK MOST ANY TYPE OF FISH WITH LITTLE PREP TIME. HAVE DINNER ON THE TABLE IN MINUTES.

SPIKE® SEASONING IS A PREPARED SEASONING AVAILABLE IN MOST GROCERY STORES. IT CONTAINS A VARIETY OF HERBS AND SPICES, SUCH AS SALT, TURMERIC, DRIED ONION, ROSEHIPS, SAFFRON AND PAPRIKA

# Balsamic Salmon

Serves: 4

## ingredients

1 pound salmon, cut into 4 four-ounce fillets

4 tablespoons Pure Maple or Blackberry Ginger Balsamic Vinegar

4 tablespoons Ultra-Premium Extra-Virgin Olive Oil

2 tablespoons fresh lemon juice, plus lemon slices for garnish

2 cloves garlic, minced

Salt to taste

## Method

Combine Ultra-Premium Extra-Virgin Olive Oil, garlic, lemon juice, Balsamic Vinegar, and salt in a small bowl. Coat salmon fillets on both sides with mixture. Place salmon in broiling pan 4" from broiler and broil for 4-6 minutes or until fish flakes. If the fish is more than 1 inch thick, you may have to turn once halfway through the broiling.

## To Serve

Plate and garnish with lemon slices. Serve immediately.

## Variations

* Place a bottle of the flavored Balsamic Vinegar used on the table for individual use. Having a pour spout in the bottle will make it easier to drizzle just the right amount desired.

* Try using a flavored olive oil with the Maple Balsamic Vinegar, such as Blood Orange, Butter or Chipotle Olive Oil. If using Blackberry Ginger Balsamic Vinegar, pair it with Tuscan Herb, Garlic, Eureka Lemon or Persian Lime Olive Oil.

SALMON IS GOOD ANY DAY OF THE WEEK. USING FLAVORED DARK BALSAMIC VINEGAR REALLY BRINGS OUT ITS RICHNESS AND ADDS A NEW DIMENSION.

# Beach 92 Fish Bake

Serves: 4

## ingredients

1–1 ½ pounds cod, cut into fillets

2 lemons, 1 juiced, 1 sliced for garnish

3 large potatoes, peeled and thinly sliced

2 leeks, medium size, sliced

6 tablespoons Wild Rosemary Olive Oil

Handful of fresh parsley, chopped, or any fresh Herb of choice, such as rosemary, chives, sage or thyme, plus extra for garnish

1 tablespoon salt

1 teaspoon pepper

## Method

Preheat oven 425°. In a large bowl, place potatoes, 4 tablespoons Wild Rosemary Olive Oil, the juice of 1 lemon, salt and pepper. Mix gently, coating the potatoes thoroughly. Place in 9x12 inch baking dish and cover with aluminum foil. Bake for 20 minutes. Take out of oven and mix ingredients. Cover and return to oven for 10 additional minutes. Set aside.

Rinse cod fillets and pat dry with paper towel. Use 2 tablespoons Wild Rosemary Olive Oil and coat both sides of the fillets. Sprinkle both sides with salt, pepper and parsley. Lay fillets over the potatoes and roast for 8 minutes uncovered. Place under broiler to lightly brown tops of fillets - approximately 3 minutes. Let rest 5 minutes.

## to Serve

Serve in baking dish, sprinkling top with fresh parsley. Garnish with lemon slices.

(Photo by Clare Hilger)

## Variations

* Substitute flavored oil, such as Eureka Lemon, Garlic, Butter, Basil, Blood Orange, or Tarragon Olive Oil.

* Add peeled, chopped cucumber for an additional fresh flavor.

THIS RECIPE IS A FAVORITE IN ROCKAWAY BEACH. EXPERIENCE A TASTE OF "ROCK-A-PULCO," AS THE LOCALS CALL IT, RIGHT IN YOUR OWN KITCHEN.

# Oven-Poached Fish with Lemon Caper Sauce

Serves: 4

## ingredients

1 ½ pounds fish of your choice, cut into fillets

5–6 tablespoons Ultra-Premium Extra-Virgin Olive Oil or flavored olive oil

3 tablespoons shallots, finely chopped

## Sauce

1 clove garlic, minced

2 tablespoons capers, rinsed and chopped

¼ cup fresh lemon juice, plus lemon quarters for garnish

3 tablespoons Ultra-Premium Extra-Virgin Olive Oil or flavored olive oil

4 tablespoons fresh parsley, finely chopped, plus extra for garnish

## Method

Preheat oven to 400°. Cover bottom of a large baking dish with oil and lay fillets flat, adding salt and pepper. Heat olive oil over medium heat in a sauté pan and add shallots. Sauté until translucent – about 3 minutes. Place shallots over fish. Cover with aluminum foil and place in oven for 8–10 minutes or until the fish is opaque and pulls apart easily with a fork.

Prepare Sauce:

While the fish is in the oven, whisk together garlic, capers, lemon juice and olive oil. When the fish is done, remove from oven and transfer to a covered platter. Pour the liquid from the baking dish into the sauté pan and over a high heat and reduce liquid. Stir often adding garlic, caper mixture and parsley. Whisk together.

## To Serve

Uncover serving platter and pour sauce over the fish. Garnish with fresh lemon quarters and serve.

## Variations

\* Herbes de Provence, Garlic, Basil, Tuscan Herb, Wild Mushroom and Sage, Wild Rosemary, Blood Orange, Eureka Lemon, Persian Lime, Butter, Cilantro, and Roasted Onion Olive Oil are good choices for this dish.

\* For a tropical taste, add a splash of Coconut Balsamic Vinegar and use Persian Lime Olive Oil.

\* For an Asian flavor, use a splash of Lemongrass Mint Balsamic Vinegar and Cilantro and Roasted Onion Olive Oil.

POACHING GIVES FISH, SUCH AS FLOUNDER, SWORDFISH, SOLE OR SALMON, A DELICATE FLAVOR.

THE SAUCE SHOWCASES THE INTRICATE FLAVOR, AND THIS RECIPE IS ENHANCED BY USING FLAVORED OLIVE OILS IN THE SAUCE. PREPARE IT WHILE THE FISH IS IN THE OVEN SO YOU'LL BE READY TO SERVE SOON AFTER YOU TAKE IT OUT.

# Tuna Ashingdon

THIS COMES FROM ACROSS THE POND AND IS THE EASIEST TUNA RECIPE IN THE WORLD! QUICK TO PREPARE AND SO TASTY.

Serves: 4

## ingredients

1 pound fresh ahi tuna steaks
⅛ cup Eureka Lemon Olive Oil
Juice of 1 lemon, plus lemon quarters for garnish
Salt and Pepper to taste

## Method

Place olive oil in skillet and heat until very hot. Place tuna in skillet, cover with lemon juice, and sear 1 ½ minutes on each side.

## To Serve

Place on serving plate and garnish with lemon quarters. Serve immediately.

## Variations

* This can be served alone or over salad, pasta, vegetables or rice.

* Garlic or Persian Lime Olive Oil can be used for a more intense flavor.

# VEGETABLES

# Best Roasted Beets

Serves: 4

## ingredients

3 medium beets, peeled and cut into large cubes

1 large sweet onion, cut into chunks

¼ cup Champagne Balsamic Vinegar

¼ cup Herbes de Provence Olive Oil

2 cloves fresh garlic, finely minced

1 teaspoon dried thyme

1 teaspoon salt

Freshly ground pepper to taste

## Method

Preheat oven to 400°. Cut the peeled beets into bite-sized cubes. Spread in a single layer on a baking sheet. In a small bowl, whisk together the Champagne Balsamic Vinegar, Herbes de Provence Olive Oil, garlic, thyme, salt, and pepper. Drizzle mixture over beets, and then toss to coat. Roast for 45–55 minutes or until beets are tender.

## To Serve

Remove from the oven and serve immediately.

## Variations

* Chill beets and mix with ¼ cup crumbled feta cheese. Drizzle with Champagne Balsamic. For a savory taste, use Ultra-Premium Extra-Virgin Olive Oil and Lemongrass Mint Balsamic Vinegar.

* Save the beet tops and wash and drain. Sauté in a couple of tablespoons of Ultra-Premium Extra-Virgin or flavored Olive Oil, adding salt and pepper, and you have another tasty, healthy side.

BEETS ARE SO PRETTY AND COME IN A VARIETY OF COLORS. NO MATTER WHICH VARIETY USED, THIS RECIPE IS SURE TO PLEASE. THEY CAN BE SERVED WARM OR COLD.

# Hazelnut Asparagus

Serves: 4

## Ingredients

2 pounds asparagus, tough ends snapped off and discarded, peeled if outer layer seems tough

⅓ cup hazelnuts, roasted

4 tablespoons flavored Olive Oil, such as Persian Lime, Grapefruit, Blood Orange, or Eureka Lemon Olive Oil

Salt and pepper to taste

> ASPARAGUS CAN BE ROASTED WITH JUST A LITTLE ULTRA-PREMIUM EXTRA-VIRGIN OLIVE OIL OR WITH FLAVORED OLIVE OIL DRIZZLED ON THEM. ANY OF THE CITRUS FLAVORED OILS GIVES THIS DISH A SPECIAL BURST OF FLAVOR.

## Method

Preheat oven 400°. Place hazelnuts in roasting pan and toast for about 5 minutes, or until lightly browned. Set aside. Using the same pan, place the prepared asparagus and drizzle with 2 tablespoons of olive oil, salt and pepper. Toss and coat evenly. Roast for 6–8 minutes until tender. Remove from oven.

## To Serve

Place asparagus on serving dish. Scatter hazelnuts on top. Drizzle with dressing recipe below. Serve immediately.

## Dressing

Whisk together reserved juices and remaining 2 tablespoons of olive oil. Season with salt and pepper.

## Variations

* Can be served on a bed of arugula or other greens for a heartier side option.

* Substitute toasted walnuts or pistachio nuts

* Flavored oils, such as Basil, Tarragon, Garlic, Eureka Lemon, Persian Lime, Grapefruit or Blood Orange Olive Oils, are delicious on asparagus. Combining two whole fruit fused oils, such as half Eureka Lemon and half Blood Orange, makes for a sparkling citrusy dressing.

* A ½-teaspoon of Roasted Walnut Oil will enhance the nutty flavor of this dish.

# Sunburst Squash

Serves: 4

## ingredients

1 ½ pounds sunburst squash, sliced into ½ inch slices

5 tablespoons Tuscan Herb Olive Oil, plus a little more for drizzling

Salt to taste

Coarse ground pepper to taste

## Method

Combine sliced squash, 2 tablespoons olive oil, salt and pepper in large bowl. Toss to coat evenly. Heat remaining oil in skillet over medium heat. Add squash and sauté 5-7 minutes. Take care not to overcook - squash should be tender but not soft.

## to Serve

Place on serving dish, drizzle a little more olive oil on top, and sprinkle with salt and pepper. Serve immediately.

THE FLUTED EDGES OF THIS SQUASH MAKE IT A PRETTY ONE TO SERVE.

SUNBURST SQUASH, ALSO CALLED PATTY-PAN SQUASH, COMES IN YELLOW, GREEN AND WHITE.

THIS SUPER-EASY RECIPE CAN BE ENHANCED DEPENDING ON YOUR TASTE.

SEE VARIATION FOR SUGGESTIONS FOR OTHER FLAVORED OILS TO HELP CREATE A NEW DISH EVERY TIME.

## Variations

* Try using Herbes de Provence, Wild Mushroom and Sage, Garlic, Butter, Wild Rosemary, Cilantro and Roasted Onion, or Harissa Olive Oil.

* A little bit of Roasted Walnut Oil or White Truffle Olive Oil will elevate this simple squash to new heights.

# Super Spinach

So good for you and so delicious, especially when you use flavored olive oil.

Serves: 4

## ingredients

1 ½ pounds baby spinach leaves

2 tablespoons Ultra-Premium Extra-Virgin Olive Oil or flavored olive oil

4 cloves garlic, chopped

2 teaspoons salt

¾ teaspoons ground black pepper

1 teaspoon butter or ¾ teaspoon Butter Olive Oil

½ lemon, juiced

Salt to taste

## Method

Use pre-packaged washed and dried spinach or rinse spinach in cold water and spin dry. In a large skillet, heat oil and sauté garlic over medium heat for about 1 minute. Add spinach, salt and pepper and toss together. Cover and cook for 2 minutes. Uncover the pan, turn the heat on high, and cook the spinach for another minute, stirring until the spinach is wilted.

## To Serve

Lift the spinach to a serving bowl and drizzle with lemon juice, Butter Olive Oil and a sprinkling of salt. Serve hot.

## Variation

Try any flavored oil that suits you, such as Garlic, Basil, Wild Rosemary, Persian Lime, or Eureka Lemon Olive Oil for starters.

# Balsamic Green Beans

Serves: 4

## ingredients ⌒

1 pound fresh, thin green beans, trimmed

8 ounces pearl onions, white, red or a mixture of both. Or 1 package frozen pearl onions, thawed

¼ cup Champagne Balsamic Vinegar

1 tablespoons butter or 2 ¼ teaspoons Butter Olive Oil

3 tablespoons Wild Mushroom and Sage Olive Oil

1 teaspoon fresh thyme, chopped, plus a couple of sprigs for garnish

Fresh sage, 2-3 sprigs for garnish - optional

¾ teaspoon salt

¾-1 teaspoon black pepper

2 teaspoons Dijon mustard

## Method

Preheat oven to 400°. In a nonreactive saucepan, combine 2 tablespoons Champagne Balsamic Vinegar, butter or Butter Olive Oil, 1 tablespoon Wild Mushroom and Sage Olive Oil, thyme, salt and pepper. Stir over medium heat until butter melts or mixture is heated through. Add onions and toss. Spread in a single layer on a baking sheet and roast for 30 minutes, stirring often, until evenly browned.

Meanwhile, in a large pot of boiling salted water, blanch green beans until just tender, about 4 minutes. Drain and rinse with cold water. Set aside.

In a large bowl, combine 2 tablespoons Wild Mushroom and Sage Olive Oil, Dijon mustard, remaining 2 tablespoons Balsamic Vinegar and salt and pepper to taste. Add beans and onions and toss well. Transfer to a covered casserole, cover and bake 20 minutes or until heated through.

## to Serve

Place in serving dish. Garnish with fresh thyme and/or sage.

## Variation

* Use Premium White Balsamic Vinegar for a lighter flavor and look.

* Or, combine Tuscan Herb Olive Oil and Red Apple Balsamic Vinegar for an herbaceous fruity flavor.

THE DARK CHAMPAGNE BALSAMIC VINEGAR CREATES A BIT OF A GLAZE, ESPECIALLY ON THE ONIONS, AND GIVES THE GREEN BEANS A RICH, COMPLEX FLAVOR.

# Quick Collards

Collards are so easy to fix. And they don't have to take hours to cook. Buy the prewashed bags, and in a few minutes you have the benefit of a delicious, fresh and healthy veggie. Cooked collards will keep in the refrigerator in a sealed container, so there's no excuse for not eating your greens.

(Photo by Clare Hilger)

Serves: 4

## Ingredients

1 large bunch fresh collard greens, deveined, chopped and rinsed or 1 bag prewashed, deveined and cut fresh collard greens – 10 ounces

3 tablespoons Ultra-Premium Extra-Virgin Olive Oil or flavored olive oil

2 tablespoons Traditional Dark Balsamic Vinegar

1 fresh lemon – ½ teaspoon lemon zest, and lemon wedges for garnish

2–3 cloves fresh garlic, finely chopped

Salt and pepper to taste

## Method

Using medium heat, heat Ultra-Premium Extra-Virgin Olive Oil in a Dutch oven. Add collards and stir to coat. Sprinkle with salt and pepper to taste and stir for about 2 minutes. Add Traditional Dark Balsamic Vinegar and mix. Sauté approximately 5 minutes to maintain green color.

## To Serve

Place on serving plate and top with lemon zest. Garnish with lemon wedges.

## Variations

* Try using kale instead of collard greens. Use Blood Orange, Garlic, Basil, Chipotle, Herbes de Provence, Tuscan Herb, Wild Rosemary, Eureka Lemon, Butter or Tarragon Olive Oil. Roasted Sesame or Roasted Walnut is a hit on greens.

* Flavored Balsamic Vinegars can be used too, such as Red Apple, Pomegranate, Dark Chocolate, Blackberry Ginger, Honey Ginger, Sicilian Lemon, Oregano, or Tangerine Balsamic Vinegar.

# DESSERTS

# Perfect Pound Cake

Serves: 10

## ingredients

5 cups all-purpose flour
½ pound butter or ¾ cup Butter Olive Oil
2 cups sugar
4 eggs
1 teaspoon salt
5 teaspoons baking powder
1 tablespoon mace or ½ tablespoon nutmeg
2 cups milk
2 teaspoons vanilla extract

## Glaze

1 cup confectioners sugar
¼ cup orange juice
Zest of one orange

Whisk ingredients together to form a thick glaze that is pourable. Drizzle cake with glaze. Let set before serving.

## Method

Pre-heat oven 350°. Grease a 10-inch tube pan, dust with flour, tapping out excess flour. In a large bowl, combine flour, salt, baking powder, mace or nutmeg together. Set aside. In a medium bowl, using a mixer, combine butter or Butter Olive Oil and sugar. While beating, add eggs one at a time. Add the flour mixture and milk, alternating the two, mixing well on low speed, then mix in the vanilla extract.

Pour into tube pan and bake for 1 hour, 30 minutes, or until toothpick comes out clean from center of cake. Cool in pan 30 minutes. Turn on rack to cool completely before glazing.

## to Serve

Place on cake stand or plate and serve warm or at room temperature.

## Variations

* This cake can be topped with a glaze or dusted with confectioners sugar.

* May serve with ice cream and drizzled with Cinnamon Pear, Pomegranate, Red Apple, Dark Espresso Balsamic Vinegar, or other Dark Balsamic Vinegar of your choice.

* Try Blood Orange, Eureka Lemon or Persian Olive Oil for a fruity flavor.

This cake can be served warm or at room temperature. Slice and toast it and drizzle a little Butter Olive Oil on top and enjoy it with a cup of tea or coffee. Wrapped well, it lasts for several days in the refrigerator.

# Banana-Fanna Blueberry Bread

Serves: 8

## ingredients —

2 cups all-purpose flour

1½ teaspoons baking powder

¼ teaspoon salt

¾ cup sugar

3 tablespoons Butter Olive Oil

2 large very ripe bananas, mashed

1 egg

1 teaspoon vanilla extract

1⅓ cups fresh blueberries

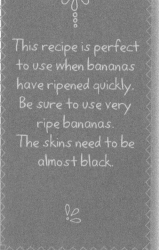

This recipe is perfect to use when bananas have ripened quickly. Be sure to use very ripe bananas. The skins need to be almost black.

## Method

Preheat oven 350°. Grease and flour 9x5 loaf pan. In a medium bowl, mix flour, baking powder and salt. In a large bowl, whisk sugar, olive oil, egg, vanilla and mashed bananas until smooth. Add in flour mixture and combine gently. Fold in blueberries using a spatula, then pour into prepared pan.

Bake approximately 55 minutes. You may need to cover with aluminum foil during the last 30 minutes to prevent over-browning. Use a toothpick to check center for doneness. Cool in pan for 10 minutes. Turn onto rack to cool completely.

## To Serve

Slice and serve warm or at room temperature. Drizzle with Blueberry Balsamic Vinegar for added blueberry flavor or Tahitian Vanilla for a smooth vanilla taste.

## Variation

Substitute Blood Orange or Eureka Lemon Olive Oil for Butter Olive Oil, or use half of each and enjoy the flavor.

# Dark Espresso Balsamic Truffles

Makes about 20–30 depending on size

## ingredients

2 tablespoons Dark Espresso Balsamic Vinegar

10 ounces high-quality 60% cocoa bittersweet chocolate chips

1 can sweetened condensed milk, 14 ounces

1 teaspoon vanilla extract

3 tablespoons unsalted butter, softened

½ cup unsweetened cocoa

## Method

In a microwave-safe bowl, combine all ingredients except cocoa and stir. Microwave 1 minute. Stir and microwave an additional 30 seconds. Remove from microwave, stir and set aside.

Prepare an 8x8 inch pan, greased and lined with waxed paper. Make sure the edges of the waxed paper extend out over two sides of the pan. Pour mixture in pan and refrigerate at least 2 hours. When firm but moldable, scoop out a small portion with a teaspoon and shape into balls the size of a large cherry. Set on waxed paper. Place cocoa powder in a shallow bowl and roll truffles in the powder until all are coated. Set on waxed paper until ready to serve.

## To Serve

Place in small paper candy cups or place a white paper doily on a serving plate.

These tiny morsels have a tangy-fruity flavor that will almost melt in your mouth. And, they can be made in advance and refrigerated or frozen until ready to serve. For best results, use the highest quality chocolate chips possible.

## Variations

\* Try Raspberry, Tahitian Vanilla or Dark Chocolate Balsamic Vinegar.

\* Coat in chopped nuts, such as roasted walnuts or hazelnuts, toasted coconut or confectioners sugar.

\* The mixture can be made in advance and refrigerated, covered in saran wrap, and stored overnight. The finished truffles will keep in an air-tight container in the refrigerator or freezer for up to two weeks.

# Grilled Peaches

Serves: 4

## ingredients

4 peaches, cut in half, remove pit
¾–1 cup Dark Espresso Balsamic Vinegar
2 tablespoons brown sugar
Vanilla ice cream, 4 scoops
Fresh mint for garnish

## Method

Cut peach in half, remove the pit. Drizzle Dark Espresso Balsamic Vinegar over peach halves. Top with brown sugar to taste. Place peaches on the grill or broil in the oven until the Balsamic Vinegar and brown sugar caramelize.

## to Serve

Place peaches on individual plates. Top with a scoop of ice cream. Garnish with fresh mint.

This dessert is easy to put together and makes a pretty presentation.

## Variations

* Strawberry, Raspberry, or Peach Balsamic Vinegar is delicious with this too.

* Pineapple, nectarines, and pears can be used instead of peaches.

* Flavored ice cream, such as peach or coffee, makes this extra-yummy.

# Last Minute Brownies

Serves: 8

## ingredients

1 package good quality Double-Chocolate Brownie Mix
Blood Orange Olive Oil

## Method

Follow brownie mix directions but instead of using vegetable oil, use Blood Orange Olive Oil. Bake as directed.

## To Serve

Good enough to serve on its own. Can add a dollop of whipped cream or a scoop of ice cream on the side.

## Variation

Try Chipotle Olive Oil for a little kick or Butter Olive Oil for a very rich, moist brownie.

Need a quick dessert?

Done!

# Old School Chocolate Cake

Serves: 8

## ingredients

2 cups sugar

1 ¾ cups all purpose flour

¾ cup unsweetened cocoa

1 ½ teaspoons baking powder

1 ½ teaspoons baking soda

1 teaspoon salt

2 eggs

1 cup milk

½ cup Ultra-Premium Extra-Virgin Olive Oil, mild

2 teaspoons vanilla extract

1 cup boiling water

Confectioners sugar to dust top if not using frosting

## Method

Preheat oven 350°. Brush two 9-inch round baking pans with olive oil and dust with flour, tapping out excess flour. In a large bowl, combine dry ingredients. Add eggs, milk, olive oil and vanilla and beat on medium speed for about 2 minutes. Stir in boiling water. Batter will be thin. Pour into pans. Bake 30–35 minutes or until wooden tooth pick inserted in center comes out clean. Cool 10 minutes. Remove from pans to wire racks and cool completely before frosting.

## To Serve

Dust with confectioners sugar. Or use the following frosting recipe. If not serving immediately, store in refrigerator.

## Variations

* If not frosted, drizzle with Dark Chocolate, Raspberry, Strawberry, or Fig Balsamic Vinegar.

* Use flavored olive oil, such as Chipotle, Blood Orange, or Butter Olive Oil to give this traditional chocolate cake a new taste.

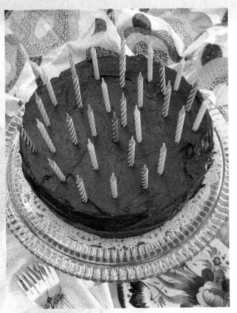

(Photo by Michele Senac)

# Chocolate Frosting

### Ingredients

½ cup butter

⅔ cup unsweetened cocoa

3 cups confectioners sugar

⅓ cup milk

1 teaspoon vanilla

### Method

Melt butter and stir in cocoa. Add confectioners sugar and milk,
alternately, beating on medium speed until it is spreading consistency.
If too thick, add a little more milk. Stir in vanilla.

### To Serve

Spread frosting on cake and serve.

Chocolate cake is the perfect dessert or birthday cake. This recipe is a variation of the traditional chocolate cake recipe that is sometimes on the back of cans of baking cocoa, only with a healthy and tasty addition – Ultra-Premium Extra-Virgin Olive Oil.

# Lime-Light Cupcakes

Makes 12

## ingredients

2 cups flour

2 ½ teaspoons baking powder

½ teaspoon salt

1 cup low-fat plain yogurt

⅔ cup sugar

½ cup Persian Lime Olive Oil

2 eggs

3 limes – zest of one lime, juice of both, plus one for garnish

1 small bottle of green sprinkles - optional

This easy dessert looks so festive. The yogurt makes the cupcakes light and moist. The Pomegranate Balsamic Vinegar icing pairs perfectly with the Persian Lime Olive Oil flavor.

## Method

Preheat oven 350°. Line cupcake pan with 12 liners. In a small bowl, combine flour, baking powder and salt and sift. Set aside. In a large bowl mix by hand yogurt, olive oil, sugar, the zest of one lime, and lime juice. Add the eggs one at a time, mixing thoroughly. Slowly stir the flour mixture in and mix until it is a creamy batter. Fill cupcake liners about ⅔ full. Bake 20 minutes or until toothpick comes out of center clean. Remove from oven and cool on wire rack.

## To Serve

Once cool, spread icing on cupcakes. Add sprinkles and garnish with lime slices. If not serving immediately, store in refrigerator.

## Variations

* Top with lime gumdrops or for holidays, top with red ones.

* Try the icing recipe using other flavored Balsamic Vinegars, such as Raspberry, Strawberry, or Black Cherry Balsamic Vinegar.

* Try using Eureka Lemon, Blood Orange, or Red Grapefruit Olive Oil in the cupcake recipe.

* For another simple cupcake recipe, see the chapter Lagniappe.

(Photo by Michele Senac)

# Pomegranate Icing

## Ingredients

1 cup heavy cream
¼ cup sugar
1 ½ tablespoons Pomegranate Balsamic Vinegar

## Method

Combine all ingredients. Using a hand mixer on medium speed, beat for about 5 minutes or until cream peaks.

## To Serve

Ice the cupcakes, garnish with sprinkles and lime slices, and serve.

# Lagniappe—A Little Something Extra

\* For a simple dessert, a scoop of ice cream with a drizzle of any flavored Dark Balsamic Vinegar of your choice makes a great presentation and is delicious. For an added touch, garnish with a mint sprig or fresh fruit.

\* For another super-simple dessert, make or purchase mini cupcakes. Create a small cavity in the center of each cupcake. Drizzle in flavored balsamic vinegar of your choice. Top with whipped cream, a few nuts or sprinkles, and a cherry.

\* Adding a splash of flavored White Balsamic Vinegar to water turns a plain glass of water into a tasty drink. Try Coconut, Pineapple, Sicilian Lemon, Cranberry Pear, Apricot or any other flavored White Balsamic Vinegar.

\* For a very refreshing drink, make "spa water." Combine ice, water, lime or lemon slices, sliced cucumbers and any flavored White Balsamic Vinegar. Place some fennel fronds in the water for a tasty and pretty appearance.

\* Gourmet croutons are simple to make and add nice texture to salad. Cut a loaf of crusty bread into 1 inch cubes and drizzle with about ½ cup of flavored olive oil of your choice. Coat thoroughly and place in 375° oven and bake for about 35 minutes, stirring occasionally so all the cubes toast evenly.

\* Toast pecan halves in a 350° oven, drizzle with your favorite Extra-Virgin Olive Oil and sea salt and serve for a quick snack.

\* Any recipe that calls for either olive oil or balsamic vinegar can be changed into a taste sensation by substituting flavored olive oil or flavored balsamic vinegar in place of plain oil and vinegar. Let your creativity flow.

For instant hors d'oeuvres, have on hand some store-bought morsels that can be served in a few minutes, such as:

* Pincholene olives, jarred or from the grocery store olive bar. Place olives in a bowl and add a drizzle of Blood Orange Olive Oil or Wild Rosemary Olive Oil. Mix and garnish with either orange zest or fresh or dried rosemary. Have some toothpicks on hand for easy serving.

* Purchase a container of Bocconcine in water, which are bite-size balls of mozzarella cheese, and drain. Place on a serving plate, drizzle with olive oil, crushed red pepper and herbs. Try Basil, Tuscan Herb, Wild Mushroom and Sage, Garlic or Wild Rosemary Olive Oil. Sprinkle with fresh or dried herbs, such as parsley, basil, thyme or oregano. Add toothpicks to serve.

* Try this simple Mediterranean snack: Slice a baguette into rounds, arrange on platter and sprinkle with robust Ultra-Premium Extra-Virgin Olive Oil, coarse ground salt and serve. Or add some crumbled feta cheese on top and serve.

* Any hard cheese, such as American Grana, Asiago, Parmesan, or Romano tastes delicious with Balsamic Vinegar. Place a wedge of cheese on a plate or cheese tray with a cheese knife and drizzle with Traditional Dark Balsamic Vinegar. Serve with rounds of bread or crackers.

* Take a wedge of brie and cover with Fig Balsamic. Serve with crackers. You're a gourmet!

* Keep a balsamic vinegar reduction on hand for an extra special flavor burst for just about any dish.

Lagniappe (pronounced lan-yap) is a French word with Cajun and Creole origins, used often in Louisiana. It means "a little something extra." Lagniappe can be something as simple as an extra beignet with your order, a second scoop of ice cream, a little extra shrimp tossed in with your meal, or as in this book, a little something extra in addition to the complete recipes.

# PART THREE
# PUTTING IT ALL TOGETHER

One of the many things my mother taught me in the kitchen was attention to details. Using good, fresh ingredients was a priority. She knew the importance of a healthy life and prepared meals using the best ingredients she could afford. Her devotion to using pure, good quality olive oil was demonstrated by the fine taste of everything she cooked. She believed in keeping the menu simple, with plenty for everyone.

Yet, her starting point was setting the table. The table was set first, and then she began to prepare a meal. She believed that a well-set table contributed to the taste and enjoyment of food. My mother paid attention to detail, making sure that everything that was needed for the meal was there. When family and friends gathered at the table, everyone could relax, unwind and enjoy the meal. Conversation flows, sharing and connection occurs, when the surroundings are relaxed. When the table feels comfortable, family and friends tend to linger to converse and share, and lingering around the table helps strengthen relationships.

Don't wait for dinner guests to come to set a nice table. Take my mother's advice and pay attention to details and set the best table you can for you and your family at every meal. Prepare a good meal, using the freshest and best ingredients you can afford, and share it with those you love.

This tradition has been around for a long time. Begin to create your own tradition — It's As Old As Time.

# ACKNOWLEDGMENTS

Many thanks to my friend, Sandy Burn, for her encouragement, knowledge, support and generosity of heart throughout this project.

Gratitude to my friend, Jackie Willey, for recipe input, for sharing her imaginative use of olive oils and vinegars, and for her expert proof reading and editing.

A hearty thank you to my son, Jeremy Jones, and my brother-in-law, Roger Fisher, for preparing and adding their own culinary touches to the meat and marinade recipes.

Grazie to my sister, Mena Scialli, for enthusiastically compiling and formatting the initial recipes in quick order, and for her time spent cooking and testing recipes.

Appreciation to my daughter-in-law, Clare Hilger, for her amazing skills in the kitchen preparing and photographing recipes and for her artistic talents in making all of the photographs come to life.

Molte bene to my sister, Lorrie Castellano, for her food styling genius, fancy photography skills, for preparing and photographing innumerable recipes on short notice and in record time, and for her invaluable input every step of the way.

# ABOUT THE AUTHOR

Michele Castellano Senac lives, writes and cooks in Greenville, South Carolina. She is a Registered Nurse with a passion for healthy living. She was inspired to write *As Old As Time*, her second book, because of her love of olive oil and balsamic vinegar and the beneficial effects these extraordinary foods have had on her life.

# INDEX

CPSIA information can be obtained
at www.ICGtesting.com
Printed in the USA
BVHW052133200220
572696BV00001B/1

9 780692 305348